EXACT FARE ONLY 2

Exact Fare Only 2

Good, Bad and Ugly Rides on Public Transit

EDITED BY

IAN COCKFIELD

INDEPENDENT PUBLISHERS

ANVIL PRESS • VANCOUVER

CANADIAN CATALOGUING IN PUBLICATION DATA

Main entry under title:

Exact fare only 2: good, bad & ugly rides on public transit / Ian Cockfield, editor.

ISBN 1-895636-55-8

1. Local transit—Anecdotes. 2. Commuting—Anecdotes. I. Cockfield, Ian 1965-
HE4211.E92 2003 388.4 C2003-911021-4

Cover: Rayola Graphic Design
Printed and bound in Canada

Teresa McWhirter's story "Another One Rides the Bus" was previously published in *Bust* magazine, Spring 2000.

Represented in Canada by the Literary Press Group
Distributed by the University of Toronto Press

The publisher gratefully acknowledges the financial assistance of the B.C. Arts Council, the Canada Council for the Arts, and the Book Publishing Industry Development Program (BPIDP) for their support of our publishing program.

BRITISH COLUMBIA ARTS COUNCIL
Supported by the Province of British Columbia

The Canada Council for the Arts | Le Conseil des Arts du Canada

Anvil Press
P.O. Box 3008, Main Post Office
Vancouver, B.C. V6B 3X5
CANADA

CONTENTS

WATCH YOUR STEP

NO LOITERING

WELCOME TO YOU FOR YOUR VISIT

NON-TRANSFERABLE

AFTERWORD

For my part, I travel not to go anywhere, but to go. I travel for travel's sake. The great affair is to move.

—Robert Louis Stevenson,
Travels with a Donkey, 1879

The poetry of motion! The real *way to travel! The* only *way to travel! Here today—in next week tomorrow! Villages skipped, towns and cities jumped—always somebody else's horizon!*

—Kenneth Grahame,
The Wind in the Willows, 1908

INTRODUCTION

Four years ago, after landing a job at a community college in the suburbs of Vancouver, I found myself part of that grudging horde of humanity: public transit users. For two hours a day I was a prisoner of that confined, public space—first a bus, then a train—and all the waiting it entailed. I read a lot, stared blankly out the window, avoided people's eyes, and learned more than I ever wanted to about strangers I would never see again. I began carrying a pocket-sized diary around so I could write down observations, anecdotes, snippets of conversation—all good fodder for a writer.

I made a note of the silent Asian immigrant in a filthy windbreaker and purple cords who shuffled down the aisle of the SkyTrain one day with a cardboard sign, "Lucky Fish 99¢," holding out origami carp made of flattened cigarette foil. (Later, on the way back home, I saw the sign and leftover fish dumped in the station's trash.) I recorded two pre-teens on a bus, one with lime-green braces, the other wearing a visor reading "Sexy," calling each other "Two-dollar whores." I witnessed the thug flashing the open Budweiser under his coat to the old woman beside him—"Working man's simple pleasure, Ma'am"—before turning back to his friend to finish the story of his six months in the youth detention centre. And then there was the stylish woman on the train dressed lavishly in black designer wear, a diamond the size of a pea on her engagement ring. After removing her cell phone and make-up kit from her purse, she pulled out an amethyst pendulum on a gold chain which she proceeded to dangle over her lap. The pendulum began to swing in tight, counter-clockwise circles, causing her some dismay. She hastily put it back in her purse. A few minutes later, she was nabbed by the ticket cops for fare evasion.

After a while, I came to realize that what I had ended up with was a collection of brief plebeian epiphanies, tiny moments of workaday clarity. Although on the surface public transit is all about destination, the writers in this follow-up collection of commuter literature remind us that it is just as much about the journey itself. For the receptive, public transit is a cultural microcosm filled with all the fear, hope, and ennui life has to offer. Whether it's the autolalic lady in the B-52's wig berating passengers—"You're diseased, you shouldn't laugh"—or the cheery "Hello" of a bus driver lifting you out of a dull midweek morning, the public transit user is continually ambushed by others and events beyond their control.

The stories, poems, and articles presented here reflect the manifold experiences public transit affords. There are the connections between people, those glimpses of possibility that often become the stories you tell friends over drinks. And so we have Elaine Miller's tale of a menacing stalker, while Karin Konoval's encounter with an overweight screenwriter on an

Arizona bus leaves her feeling blessed. Social commentary and wry observation form the basis of Matt Hern's story of a funked-out Chicago gangsta and an indiscreet disabled man, as does Marc Boudignon's visceral account of a late-night ride on a Toronto streetcar during a thunder storm. And since public transit is a global phenomenon, its various incarnations elsewhere in the world are explored: Stephen Johnson relates the much needed diversion provided by subway buskers in reunified Berlin, while Jeremiah Aherne takes us on a romp to the bottom of Mexico's Copper Canyon. Then there are the deeper, personal relationships people form. Nicole Bohn, a young commuter with cerebral palsy, looks for love on the San Francisco bus system, and Jacyntha England recollects being a twelve-year-old girl trying to reconnect with her dad on a B.C. ferry.

And just so you don't lose sight of the pragmatic in all of this, renowned scientist and environmental advocate, David Suzuki, states in the Afterword his case for the revitalization of public transit and its necessity for humankind—here's to less smog, quieter neighbourhoods, and more tales!

So the next time you need to go somewhere, hitch a ride on the peasant wagon. You'll be doing your part for the environment, and might just glimpse something that will make your world shine that much brighter.

Now sit back and enjoy the ride.

Ian Cockfield
Vancouver, September 2003

WATCH YOUR STEP

Another One Rides the Bus

Teresa McWhirter

I have been summoned to Ottawa, the city that spawned both Alanis Morissette and Paul Anka, for my brother's wedding. It's summertime and I don't really want to leave Vancouver, but I love free food and drinks, and most of all, my brother. I will go, but I decide to have an adventure on the way there. I have travelled across Canada three times, once with my parents, once with an ex-boyfriend, and once with friends. This time, I want to see America.

Maybe I'll find love (but I doubt it—I usually can't even find someone with rolling papers). Unfortunately, I don't have a vehicle. I can hitchhike, if I want to depend on the kindness of strangers. Being small and easy to kill, I take the bus. There is a cross-section of a culture you will only find travelling Greyhound: you can sit next to a nicotine-patch-wearing housewife complaining of her three ungrateful children, or a businessman with gastrointestinal problems. I love road trips, and I'm good at them, too. I rarely wash my hair and can stare blankly at one spot for hours. A four-day bus ride across America should get me in prime condition to puke up champagne and flash my relatives. I can't wait.

Los Angeles

I fly into LAX and find a hostel on Hollywood Boulevard. I meet a biker named Dirty Jerry who tells me his Harley was filmed in *Pretty Woman*. He also warns me to avoid the L.A. bus depot at all costs. Dirty Jerry tells me to avoid the city buses as well, but what's a poor traveller to do? I take the bus back from Venice Beach to the hostel room I share with eight Australian rugby players who have regarded me suspiciously ever since I fixed the toilet. Naturally, I am in no hurry to return. A fat man in the back of the bus keeps singing, "Jesus! I love ya! Woo-hoo!" Then he shits his pants. The smell is unbearable but no one says a word, although I do see a man pull out some kind of aerosol can and spray discreetly.

Las Vegas

I get a ride to Las Vegas with a South African named Heiney (I kid you not). Heiney drops me off at the bus depot in north Vegas. As I have addiction issues, I'm not allowed to gamble and it's a good thing because the smell of desperation sticks like sweat. The line at the counter snakes chaotically; everyone looks beat up and broke, or worse. A young man with sores on his lips asks if I have been to the El Cortez. I tell him

I have no money to gamble and he writes down an address where I can donate blood for twenty dollars, which includes free cookies and juice. He tells me to get there before 6 a.m. or I won't get in. I just want to get on the bus. When I finally get to the front of the line, I tell the ticket agent I want to go to Toronto and she snaps, "Where's that? We don't go there!" After much persuasion, I get her to check the computer. I spell Ontario three times.

DENVER

We pass through Beaver, Utah, and I am particularly bummed that I didn't have time to get a T-shirt. The Denver bus depot is large and sterile, with the feel of a recreational facility with no fun equipment. The gift shop is filled with sports memorabilia but does not sell aspirin, stamps, or batteries. Naturally there is a McDonald's nearby. Back on the bus I take the last available seat, beside a homeboy from Baltimore who looks scary and so no one wants to sit with him. I offer to share my fries and he gives me some candies his auntie packed in a lunch. I have finally made a friend.

OMAHA

The cafeteria cashier in the depot warns me that Omaha is a very rough place. The bus station smells like cigarettes and feels like a bingo hall. Though I don't think of Nebraska as a war zone, I do agree we live in a culture of menace. At the café across the street a fat policeman eats pie and laughs with the cook. As I sit there, two Latino boys from the bus come in. The cook watches them and when they're settled he approaches them and says, "Don't steal the silverware, amigos." I finish my tea in silent shame.

The bus breaks down on the way to Des Moines. After an hour, a mutiny is brewing. Passengers begin to complain loudly. Suddenly a man with an Afro gets up as if to make a speech. He tells us we will be fine and "America is Gemini rising." A few minutes later, we are moving. The man with the Afro throws out his arms and yells that he loves us all. Everyone claps. This never happens on buses in Canada.

Cleveland

During the two-hour stopover, I play Ms. Pac-Man with a cute boy and win repeatedly. "You're sharking me," says the hotcake, which pleases me immensely. Outside smoking a cigarette, a man says he will pay a quarter if he can smell my bum. The bus depot is antiseptic green and the bathroom is on the second floor. I make this trek four times with all my gear. I vow to stop drinking so much fruit juice. A man tries to sell me hash but I tell him I'm going to cross the border. He yells, "I'm not talking about a brick or anything!" I debate, but my drug paranoia at border crossings is far greater than the boredom of another ten hours on the bus.

Toronto

I get off the bus in Toronto with an attitude. The depot is cool and clean and everyone speaks in whispers. On my last bus ride, to Ottawa, I watch people pretend to sleep so they don't have to share a seat. In this country, according to the strict rules of Canadian politeness, anything unpleasant is ignored. And I don't smell so good.

I don't care. I've just come from my American road trip, and I've got some new stories to tell. So I didn't find love on the Greyhound Express, big deal. I think how relaxing it is to not have to decipher the looks of strangers, but that is why I love America: Anything can happen.

Follow That Bus!

Elaine Miller

I was waiting for the Number 152 bus at the stop at Commercial and Hastings on a balmy evening in early fall. And waiting. And waiting. I desperately wished to be home already, to take off my constricting office clothing and climb into my comfy bed, but even if the bus arrived at that second it would still be thirty dreary minutes before it reached my stop in the 'burbs. I shifted from one aching foot to the other, and fiddled with my belongings as I wondered in which of my bags I had placed my half-read science fiction book. As I found the novel and fished it out with a disproportionate feeling of triumph, a vaguely sporty-looking maroon sedan pulled up beside the bus stop, and the driver leaned over and spoke to me through the open passenger window. "Hi, beautiful," he said, as witty and original as are all men who attempt to pick up dates at bus stops. "Would you like a ride?"

"Uh, no thanks," quoth I, as eager to be friendly as are all tired young women at the end of a long day at work. I pointedly opened the book and intently regarded the first page I came to. This, I hoped, would end the matter.

"Would you like to go for a drink? Come on, let's just go for a drink."

"No. No, I do not want a drink." I understand the value of a firmly expressed opinion when dealing with importunate sorts. As if in solidarity, a few cars honked little polite Canadian honks behind Mr. Auto Erotica, and he cruised off slowly, with many backward looks.

Happily for my poor feet, I spotted the bus in the distance, and occupied the moments before its arrival with fishing out correct change. As I climbed aboard, a quick glance to my left showed that Mr. Auto had driven around the block—presumably for a second doomed flirting attempt—and was just turning the corner behind the bus.

I shook my head at that, and smiled to myself as I found the best reading seat on the bus. For those who haven't already figured it out, the best reading seat for a left-handed book-holder is the leftmost window seat directly behind the sideways seats at the back—the wheel hump is the perfect thing to place a foot upon; one's knee then becomes a well-positioned elbow rest. And since twilight was fast deepening into full dark, the lights at the back of the bus were important. I forgot about Mr. Auto the second I reopened my book.

Sixty pages later I yanked the pull cord as we neared my stop. After commuting for so long, I almost knew without looking which of the dark and lonely stops along the Lougheed Highway was mine. Home was now a mere ten-minute walk away, through dark woods, along the outside of the fences belonging to a town house mini-city, through a small field, and then at last through my own little mushroom-patch of town houses. I yearned for my cat and—most importantly—my bed. The bus pulled over in a crunch of gravel. I got out into the cooling night, and waited on the soft shoulder for the bus to pull back out into traffic, averting my face from its rush of wind and dust.

When I looked up, there he was, leaning over to talk to me through the passenger window again. Same guy. Same car. I took the obligatory long moment to blink stupidly, as there's been an awful lot of generations between me and the days of sabre-toothed tigers and instantaneous reactions to danger. Then my thinking brain took over the job my instincts had started: 1. No sane man follows a damn bus for thirty-three minutes in the dark; 2. Therefore this man is not sane; 3. Back there we were in public twilight, now we're on a very dark suburban highway, functionally alone as sporadic cars whisk by at 70 KPH; 4. Bad. Very bad. I'm standing alone in the dark with a complete nutter in a car staring at me.

"Need a ride? Why don't we go for that drink now?" he shouted. "Get in the car."

Nice pick-up technique, Mr. Nutter. Sweep a girl off her feet, why don't you. When in doubt, pretend to be unalarmed and stall for time. "Sorry. Can't. Gotta go home. I'm late. I'm expected. I live right in there. Bye now." I pointed at the nearest set of town houses, mentally apologizing to the unknown inhabitants. Then I turned and took off at a very brisk walk, ready to bolt the second I heard a car door open, because that meant Mr. Nutter was about to cross the line from merely obsessive to assaultive. The car stayed in place, motor running, as I trotted down the stairs of the path, and I cursed the designer of the town houses, because there was no actual way to run to the nearest house and wait for him to go away. Not unless I could scale an eight-foot solid wood fence while wearing a grey, woolen, calf-length skirt and sensible pumps.

The farther I moved from the highway, the easier I breathed, although I still had my ears pricked like a rabbit's and continued to look all about me. Which was lucky, because I spotted the car by its headlights before its driver could have been close enough to spot me. I leapt abruptly into a friendly seeming bush and watched from its leafy concealment as Mr. Nutter parked, headlights on, at the end of the cul-de-sac. He must have cleverly worked out for himself that if I was heading this way that I would have to pass right through the headlights' beams. The unbroken line of fence and the pathless trees on the other side limited my choices to two: back the way I'd come, or forward, past this cul-de-sac. So I formed a real relationship with that bush. Twenty-five minutes I crouched silently in its embrace, watching him watch for me.

For the first ten minutes, I felt the anger-driven temptation to stride in a dignified way out of the bush, and let the blood drops fall where they may if he laid a hand on me. I played with my Swiss Army knife, noting with chagrin that its largest ($2^{3/4}$-inch) blade was not very Crocodile Dundee-ish. Mr. Nutter might or might not be a psychopathic killer. At the very least he was too weird to get dates by charm and personality. He might be armed with a gun, a chainsaw—or at the very least, a knife blade longer than $2^{3/4}$ inches. I had to concede that he probably had come to the battle better armed and more prepared than I, which was no surprise as the worst fight I'd been expecting that night had been the inevitable rush for the best reading seat at the back of the bus.

For the next ten minutes, after concluding that I wouldn't attempt confrontation unless pushed to it, I had plenty of time to consider issues of feminism. That this damn testosterone-laden idiot could cause me to hide like a field mouse by virtue of his insanity, possible armed status, and almost inevitable greater muscular strength, offended me to the roots of my independent female being. It couldn't have rankled worse if I'd been crouched in poison ivy.

I thought wistful thoughts about having black-belt-level skills in some esoteric martial art, and bounding out of the bush and into the menacing Flamingo-of-Death stance. All blows struck would automatically be for the rights of women everywhere to walk safely down the street at night. Alas, I had spent more time developing my literacy skills than my pugilistic ones, although I would have gladly traded my pen for a sword right at that moment.

The rest of the time was spent, I confess, in watching him leaning on the side of his car, and wondering. I wondered what evolutionary fault would lead a gentleman to pursue a date for the night in this rather odd style. Perhaps it was an echo of the way our prehistoric ancestors would ride mastodons up to a cavechick in leopard skin and say, "Woman, get on elephant now!"

I had enough time to come up with a humorous interpretation that involved *Homo Erectus* and tiny frontal lobes, when he at last got back in his car, popped it in reverse, and headed up the cul-de-sac.

When his car reached the end of the block, I broke out of concealment at a dead run, shoes in my bag and nylons be damned. I bolted across the empty space and took a quick jig down the path through the bushes, and when I fancied I heard the returning spin of car tires, why, I simply ran faster. It's surprising how quickly one can cover ground that takes six minutes to walk at the end of each workday. Hearing my own heartbeat too loudly in the dim light, I took care to make sure no one was near as I approached my own front door, opened it as soundlessly as possible, closed it behind me in the same manner. I didn't want Mr. Homo Erectus, if he was still on the trail, to know which of the many doors in the complex I'd gone through.

If this had been a movie, I would have forgotten to chain the door or turn the deadbolt, and the creepy music would have played to let the audience know that I'd made a mistake that was about to cost me my life. But I've always been contemptuous of scriptwriters who portray woman as a creature who is too dumb to take off her pumps before running like hell. I write a more realistic script, in which we do what we need to do, in order to keep ourselves whole. And my deadbolt slid home the second my door clicked shut.

14 Hastings

Peter Norman

Flexing, cramping its accordion waist
the bus sidles up to the curb.
I am inside, immersed in the burble
of voices, slick sick jokes cracked
by two men behind me, swagger of b-boys
who jostle joust adjust
the angles of their caps,
omnivorous fear from an old woman huddled
at the front, speaking only to air.

We have stopped beside a Petro-Can.
Batwing doors fold open to accept
a hunchback. He hobbles up steps,
coins clutched in precarious fingers
& dropped
haphazard on the floor.
The driver waves him aboard, dodging
confrontation, admitting
fare was almost paid.

And the hunchback sits across the aisle from me,
propped on his seat like the crook of a cane,
limbs in constant spasm, clothes gashed,
hand-picked from bags left outside Salvation
Army depots in the rain, skin stained
with years. They could take his fingerprints
without ink.

And in one hand he clasps a rag
like it's his last possession,
holds it to his face,
to wipe his nose (I think) or dab his chin,
gouge the street from his pores.

But he presses so hard,
as if to force it through his flesh,
thrusts it like a gag into his mouth,
breathes deep, phlegm
a rattlesnake in his throat.
And then the stench begins
to billow through the bus, and I know
I've smelled that smell before, I know
that smell.

And then I know.

And I see with gruesome clarity
his hand, its twitch, oil lodged
under nails, the rag. The odour
is gasoline.

Conversations have flickered and died.
Everyone averts eyes or stares.
We move now, urban montage
sliding past windows. I lurch
to the front, tap
the driver's shoulder.

She won't look up. She's navigating
rush hour, hands rooted
at 10 and 2 o'clock on the wheel.
There's a man, I say, *can you smell it?*
He's sucking gasoline.

She turns now, looks right at me.
I'm working, she says, and glances at my feet:
You're standing over the red line.
Please step back.

Dario's Dream

Karin Konoval

It's all well and good relaxing under a palm tree until a bird shits on your head, which just happened. I'm sitting on a rock outside the Greyhound bus station in Yuma, Arizona. When I got here at 8:30 this morning they gave me the news that the ten o'clock bus for Palm Springs is full leaving Phoenix; so "Unless there's a drunk on the bus who needs to be kicked off," it's just me and my palm tree until the next bus at noon. An old man sitting on his duffel bag in the park across the street pulls out his pipe. He's in the same situation, as are five or six more people waiting inside.

When I go back into the station to clean myself up the desk clerk tells me that, due to my patience and good spirits, I've just made spot Number One on his waiting list. The ten o'clock bus pulls in and lo and behold they did indeed have to kick some drunks off. The old man with the pipe and I are chosen to come aboard. I make my way down the aisle, sullen faces assuring me that every seat is taken. I get off and tell the driver I'd rather wait for the noon bus.

He makes a face. "Yah, yah, I find you de place." He comes back a moment later. "You got de choice. Big fat guy three rows back, or wid de hoodlums in de back of de bus. Hey," he smiles, patting me on the shoulder, "eez jus' one leetle hour to Calexico."

Wishing I could stay behind, I get on the bus and sit down—or more accurately, perch—beside the largest man I've ever seen in my life, well over four hundred pounds. He's wheezing and tries to pull bits of himself from my portion of our seat.

"That's okay," I tell him.

On the way out of town our driver points out the historic Yuma territorial prison to our right and announces that we are entering California.

"YO!" yells one of the hoodlums from the back of the bus. "Remember the motherfuckin' Alamo!"

We ride across sand dunes, past cornfields where Mexican workers are bent down, their colourful hats bobbing over a sea of green. My companion, still wheezing, holds a hand out over the shelf of his stomach. "Name's Dario," he says.

"Karin," I answer. I watch as he wrestles a tub of tobacco out from somewhere underneath himself. Opening it, he pulls out a little machine and a handful of cigarette tubes. He starts making cigarettes. The loose tobacco drifts over the hills of his stomach.

"Where'd you get on?" I ask.

"Georgia," he wheezes.

"Georgia?"

Dario nods. "Yup. Been on this same bus for two days. I'm on my way to Los Angeles."

"Congratulations," I say, unable to think of anything else.

From the back of the bus the hoodlums have set up a chant. "One-two-three-four! Bang that pussy 'til it's rawr!"

"Manners, manners!" calls our driver. The hoodlums laugh and fall silent.

"I have to go home," continues Dario, making cigarettes, "because the only dream I ever had just came true."

I look at him curiously. He smiles back at me.

"I'm goin' to Hollywood!" he announces. "Hollywood finally called."

I watch him wheezing away as he tamps fingerfuls of tobacco into his little machine and struggles with its lever. I notice a nicotine patch on his right arm, see the sweat stains on his dirty T-shirt spreading out from his armpits over his womanly breasts. He appears to have no chin at all, just a bulbous mass of flesh from his lips to his collarbone. His eyes are the most startling, big and soft, with dark circles that travel all the way around them as if painted on with a smudge stick. Not meaning it unkindly, he looks like a human raccoon. Hollywood, I think to myself. I don't know whether to laugh or cry.

"My mom was an opera singer," he confides, "and my dad was a symphony conductor. They always wished I'd make something of myself. Well," he looks out the window, nodding to himself, "now I'm finally gonna do it."

"How have you enjoyed the bus trip?" I ask, changing the subject. He may be nuts, but if he is, it's in a gentle kind of way and I hurt for him.

"It's been okay," says Dario. "I've had a lot of stuff to think about, things to plan. The only thing I hate is that cubbyhole." He gestures to the back of the bus.

"The bathroom?"

"Yeah." He blushes. "I hate peeing in public. I guess you could call me 'pee shy'."

I try to imagine him squeezing out of this seat, down the aisle and into the bathroom. I can't.

"Yup, I've had a lot of things to think about," Dario goes on. "I been pinching myself all the way from Georgia. That's why I took the bus. They were gonna fly me, but I said no. I figured the excitement might give me another heart attack. This way, I can get used to the news slowly."

"You've had a heart attack before?"

"Two," he admits. "Plus there's a bunch of other stuff wrong with me I gotta get fixed before I'm a big shot in Hollywood. Then there's the other thing I've been trying to figure out all this way: Where to hide the money?"

Okay, I say to myself. You could have picked the seat with the hoodlums, but no. So now you're stuck with a mild-mannered lunatic who's just robbed a bank and thinks he's on his way to Hollywood to be a star. Glancing over my shoulder I see the old man with the pipe sitting back there between the hoodlums. One of them has his pipe and is peering into the bowl of it like a bear looking at the workings of a Swiss watch. The other one is dealing a game of cards on the old man's lap. He appears comfortable with this, politely holding his knees together so the cards don't fall and silently mouthing the deal count.

"Here." Stuffing everything into the tub of tobacco Dario somehow manages to wiggle it back underneath himself. "Wanna show you something," he says, feeling around down there.

"Oh! That's okay," I say.

"No, I want to," says Dario. "Take a look at this." He

hands me a cheque for fifteen thousand dollars from a major Hollywood studio, made out to him.

"What is this?" I ask, holding the cheque between my fingers. It's warm and slightly damp from wherever he's been keeping it.

Dario grins. "It's the down payment," he says. "For my very first screenplay in my own name."

"You're a writer? I thought—"

"That I was an *actor?*" Dario wheezes with laughter. "God, no. I wanna *make* something out of my life." He takes the cheque back. "Fifteen grand," he marvels. "Go figure, hey?"

"Congratulations," I say again. This time I mean it.

"Thanks," says Dario. "Boy, you just never know when your number's gonna come up, do you?" He traces his finger over his name on the cheque. "See? That's me right there. I still can't believe it."

"You should probably get that into the bank," I say. "It's an awful lot of money." I glance back at the hoodlums. They're still playing cards using the old man as a table. Arms folded, he seems to have fallen asleep.

"Well, that's the thing," frowns Dario. "That's the one thing I haven't figured out yet. If I put it in the bank, then it's my money. I've been on social security the last five years and I still need it. Especially for the medical, until I get myself fixed up. Then, when I'm fixed, I can afford to get rich and famous. Until then I gotta find somewhere to hide the money."

My head swims with the logic of this. "What's your screenplay about?"

"Well," says Dario, suddenly shy. "It's about—how do I explain it? You ever notice those headlines that go by on CNN?

The ones on the ticker tape under the picture that only show up once and make you go, Whoa? And you know it's a really important story, but then you never hear of it again? Well, that's what my movie is about. One of those little stories that turns out to be pretty big."

There's a hoot from the rear of the bus. Somebody must have won. I turn to see the old man wake with a start. One of the hoodlums gets out a bag of unshelled peanuts. Resting it on the old man between them the hoodlums start cracking peanuts open in their teeth, spitting the shells on the floor. One of them hands the old man a peanut; he looks at it, cracks it open in his teeth and spits the shell on the floor too. The other hoodlum hands him a peanut; he does it again. And so it goes. The old man never puts his hand in the bag, like a baby bird he just waits to be fed.

" . . . but that's the thing about ghost-writing," Dario is saying.

"Pardon?"

"I was saying about the ghost-writing, what I've been doing up 'til now. It's like I know it's me, and Frankie knows it's me. And in here." He taps his chest. "It's not just what I do, it's who I am. A writer. But when you're ghost-writing it's like you're not quite all there. Or like you're there, but you're trapped in someone else's clothes." He wiggles uncomfortably. "Man, these seats sure get to you after a while."

"Who's Frankie?" I ask.

He names a famous Frankie that I recognize. "You probably heard of his dad. I've been ghost-writing for him for years, mostly B-movie scripts. Guy doesn't have a literate bone in his body, but he's got a name. That's what counts in Hollywood, you know? Having a name."

"Yes," I agree.

"So it's good to be getting out from underneath, finally. Getting a name of my own. It's scary, but it's good. I keep seeing it in my mind, you know?" He holds his hand up to the window and spreads his fingers over the glass. "My very own name, flashing by on the credits. It won't be in big print, like the stars," he laughs, "but it'll be there. Like I really exist. Yup," he sighs, "I'm finally gonna have my own place in the sun."

At this moment the bus turns and the sun does actually hit Dario, falling across him like a benediction. I watch him caught in this beam of light, riding toward his dream. From inside the cage of his enormous man's body, the light hope of a boy looks out.

"I was thinking," says Dario, "that I'm going to take up swimming. I've lost some weight already, but I need to lose a bunch more. I don't know if you can picture it, but I used to weigh 450 pounds. I'm almost down to four hundred now." He's shy again.

"Good for you," I smile at him, wishing him well with my whole heart.

"Do you think that'd be a good idea? Do you think it would help?"

"Go for it," I say. Dario grins, pleased.

As the bus pulls into Calexico, I peek over my shoulder. Awash in a sea of peanut shells, the old man and the hoodlums have fallen asleep, their heads on each other's shoulders. Connections can happen, it seems, in the most surprising ways and places. And in a moment of possibility, we find our place in the world again. I look back at Dario. He's still grinning at me.

Making the Last Bus

Catherine McNeil

for Kim Addonizio

it’s pissin’ out ’n i miss the last bus transfer to phibb’s
exchange. i’m huffin’ it up robson. this guy appears
outside the sheraton landmark. asks me why i’m crying.
i tell him i missed my bus and i’ll be in a ship loada’
trouble if i don’t get home. he says he’ll give me a ride.
he looks okay. he looks like her. i’m in love with her
so i’ve got everybody that slightly resembles her way
up there on a pedestal. he has to run up to his hotel
room and grab his keys. “c’mon” he says. i follow.
inside his hotel room he asks me what i’ll give him.
“what do you mean?” i ask. “a quick fuck for the ride”
he says. i tell him “i’m catholic. i teach catechism. i
don’t even have a boyfriend. i can’t get pregnant.” “then
suck me off.” he whips it out pushing my head my mouth
down onto it. i’d done this before when i was twelve. at
least i’d get home soon. make that last bus. mom and dad
would be relieved.

Missed Bus

Matthew Firth

I call the Hamilton Street Railway's Bus Check number for my stop. The Stephen-Hawking-esque voice says, "Bus Check schedule. Route 7. Locke. Next bus to King Street and John Street in four minutes. Following bus in twenty-four minutes."

That automated voice never lies. It's saved me from freezing for twenty minutes at a time, staring up Dundurn Street, on many occasions. A beautiful invention, Bus Check. Way better than the old days with those hard-to-decipher paper schedules, with all their different departures depending on whether it was rush hour, a weekend, a holiday, a bloody full moon, or some such thing. I could never make sense of those schedules. But the blue-rinse grannies always could, cheekily puttering around the corner with their walkers just as the bus pulled into the stop. Bus Check just tells you what you need to know: when the next bus will arrive at *your* stop.

So I sprint out the door at exactly twenty-three minutes to midnight, thirty seconds after hanging up the phone. I live right around the corner from the stop on Dundurn Street. I know four minutes means bolt it, now!

The closest call I've had and still made it was "Next bus in two minutes." I had a "Next bus in one minute" once. I nearly dropped dead on the floor. I ran to the stop—untied shoelaces fluttering in the cold breeze—only to catch a whiff of diesel as Route 7 pulled away. Had my shoelaces been tied, I might have beat it to the next stop and boarded, but the god of public transit was conspiring against me that night.

There is nothing worse than missing a bus. I tell my girlfriend this time and time again. She just doesn't understand my urgency, my panic—she being of some sort of suave, laid-back, Eastern European, the-bus-will-get-here-when-it-gets-here mentality. She's yet to call Bus Check—probably has no idea the service exists.

Me, I'm white-knuckled when it comes to catching the bus. I like precision. Especially when getting to work on time hangs in the balance. And that's another thing: I hate getting to work early. Not even two, three minutes. That's *my* time, not theirs. I'm not selling my labour to the boss for free. Fuck the white hats. That's always been my philosophy.

So if I time the bus just right, I can step through the doors at the Wesley Centre at exactly midnight to start my shift. Of course, that's after pushing through the crowd of thugs waiting for the night program to begin—the huddled masses eager for a bowl of reheated, leftover soup ("These noodles are too soggy," someone invariably complains) and a hard bench or a hard floor to sleep on; one more night out of the cold. It's been a nasty winter so far: two dead from exposure on the city streets already.

I digress. Back to the bus. I'm safely around the corner now, semi-race-walking to the stop. But I don't hear the bus's groan as it pulls away from its perch at the top of Dundurn Street, two hundred metres or so away. That's the end of the line, where Dundurn stops at the foot of the Niagara escarpment—"The mountain" to locals. The Locke bus always makes a wide, 360-degree turn on the steep hill. The driver then sits and drinks coffee from a thermos, maybe reads the paper 'til it's time to start the run back downtown. My stop is the second on the route. You can usually see the bus sitting at the top of the street in among the trees on the side of the mountain.

So I look over my shoulder as I walk and check up the street. No bus coming. I can't even see it. It must be up there. It's supposed to be at my stop in a minute or so.

I get to the stop. My pulse quickens. Look up the street. No bus. Check my pocket for my bus pass for the two-thousandth time in my life, probably. Check the Bus Check phone number pasted to the pole, just to be certain. Look up the street. No bus. Check my watch. It's at least four minutes since I hung up the phone. What gives?

Check up the street again. No bus. Check my toque. Pull my gloves up tightly onto the cuffs of my coat. Check up the street. No bus. Check that my wallet and keys are in my pockets. Check my bus pass again. Take one glove off and check that my nuts are still hanging from my crotch. Then check up the street. Still no bus!

I look at my watch again. Six minutes since Stephen Hawking told me the bus was coming in four minutes. Fuck sakes. I'll be late for work. Once downtown, I'll have to run from Gore Park over to the Wesley Centre to make it on time.

I fidget. Kick clumps of snow on the pavement. Peer into the empty newspaper box. Being a midnight commuter there are no papers left. Look up Dundurn again. No bus in sight.

Eight minutes since Stephen Hawking. This is serious. I'll be late for sure and my supervisor will kick my ass. The clients at the centre will complain if they have to wait an extra three minutes for me to serve their soup and stale sandwiches. They'll be on my case all night, probably not relenting 'til after I serve breakfast.

It's a shit job, anyway—soup kitchen cook. Mostly I get fed nothing but grief, the clients taking out the day's frustrations on me, like anyone would, like spouses bitching at spouses at the end of the workday commute. But some of the clients are okay. And most are fast asleep by two o'clock. Once I clean up the soup and sandwiches, do the dishes, I usually get two, three hours to myself to read a book, to write a letter or two, to play chess with Harold, the guy who cleans the washrooms at the centre. Of course, that usually means putting up with Harold's attempts to convert me. He's a devout Witness. After Friday night shifts, I've seen him change out of his custodian's greens into a three-piece suit to hit the streets and save some souls.

Shit, that's ten minutes now! Something's up with this bus. I've got two choices. Cab it, which I've done in a pinch, but it's like fourteen bucks to get to the centre. Payday's a full ten days off, so that's not the most favoured option. The other choice is to investigate. Maybe the driver nodded off. Maybe his watch is broken. Maybe he has no clue what Stephen Hawking told me ten minutes ago. Maybe he still goes by the old paper schedule. Or the dude just doesn't care if I'm late for work. He likely hates the late-night shift anyway, having to deal with weirdoes, drunks, and whores all night. In some sense, I can't blame him for not wanting to start his run. We're both in the same line of work: providing essential public services to those in need.

Okay, that's eleven minutes. I can't stand here another second. But it's still a tough choice. If I leave now to run up to the top of Dundurn, the bus might suddenly lurch out from the trees. Then I'll be stranded between stops, like a mouse scrambling for cover as a hawk swoops down for the kill. I'll be screwed. I'll miss the bus and that'll be that. But I can't wait here and do nothing. The anxiety is killing me. I need to see what's up.

I sprint up the street, covering the two hundred metres in forty seconds, which isn't bad for a nearly middle-aged slug in winter boots. The bus *is* there. Only it's tucked back in the trees more than usual. The lights are on. The engine is silent. The driver's seat is empty.

I stomp over. Knock on the door. Nothing. I look up through the passenger windows. Nothing to see there from this angle but the chiropractor and gum adverts above the seats. I knock again. Nothing. Is the guy off having a shit in the woods? Maybe.

Then I hear something from inside the coach. Noises. Movement. I gotta find out what the hell is going on here. Maybe the driver's getting worked over by thugs. I jam a gloved hand between the panes of glass of the divided door, prying them apart. I wedge myself through and emerge on the other side, step up the two steps, and hear more movement. I look to my left. There's the driver, the bastard. He's taking his break all right. Taking it way too far. The dude's screwing some broad, getting a little midnight action while I get worked up down the street waiting for this bus. And he's banging her right in the first seat, the one behind the driver that's reserved for the infirm. The one the blue-rinse grannies grab. I always see them sitting there, leaning forward, watching every move the driver makes, anxious they'll miss their stop. They ring that bell the exact second the driver leaves the stop before their own. They covet those bus seats like other folk covet front row seats at a Leafs game.

The driver doesn't flinch when I come on board the bus. He's still mostly dressed, his tan polyester trousers down around his shins, his bus-driver's brown cardigan sweater dishevelled. Greasy hair messed. Dandruff on his shoulders. His white ass up in the air. He's supporting himself with one hand planted on the floor of the bus. The other is scrunched under the woman. His ass drives like a jackhammer. He must be almost finished—must know he's late for his run and wants to wrap this up.

I can barely see the woman. She's wearing fuck-me boots. The rest of her is hard to make out; she's mostly swaddled in her winter greatcoat, a kind of pukey, pea-green number. I see a tangle of peroxide-blonde hair and one grubby hand. Maybe she's working, too. Maybe she's providing an essential service as well.

And then I glance up. There's a cane resting against the seat behind the one they're screwing on. Well, what do you call this then? At least they're entitled to be in that seat. An older girl, she is.

I drag my feet. Clear my throat. Still nothing. She's likely half asleep. I see a glimmer of sweat on the back of the old boy's neck. He's really working at it, getting his money's worth. I didn't realize they paid these guys that well. Or maybe this one is off the cuff from her, in exchange for a ride downtown. No, she can't give it away for the equivalent of $1.85, can she? In exchange for a monthly bus pass? That's more likely. I'm witness to a simple exchange of services here.

I can't stand this any more. "Hey, excuse me."

His ass still pumps. No sign of life from her.

"Mr. Bus Driver. Hey!"

This time he turns his head. "What the fuck do you want?"

I can't believe this. The dude just doesn't care that I'm watching him have sex on his bus. He's obviously not shy and must have a kick-ass union to boot if he feels this secure in his job.

I can't talk to the guy like this. Or maybe I can. I traipsed all the way up here. "Uhhhmm . . . I'm late for work."

He looks back at me again, his face a bit more strained. "Yeah?" he grunts.

"I gotta get to work. You gotta get this bus in gear."

The conversation seems to have roused the woman. She peers out from beneath him. Her face is all pasted up—mascara, rouge, baby-blue eye shadow. I can't tell if she's twenty-five or fifty-five. She looks to be a working girl, though. Must be—she, too, is unbothered by my intrusion.

I point down the street. "You're late."

He slows down a bit. "No chance. I know the schedule. And besides, you ain't my boss." Then he pushes hard against her. She groans.

"I thought the general public was your boss," I fire back.

"Fuck that cliché."

I pause for a second and then start again. "But I called Bus Check. It said—"

The woman barks at me from under him. "Just let him finish, asshole!"

I'm losing my nerve. These are obviously two tough customers. They can argue and screw at the same time.

I look at the driver in his rumpled uniform. "But Bus Check said—"

He turns and glares at me one last time. "Will you please just piss off! Can't you see I'm busy? Get the hell off my bus!"

I think this does it for him. He lets out a gasp and crumples on top of the woman. She sighs faintly, relieved that it's over.

That's it, I've had it. I'm not waiting around for their post-coital exchange. This is too weird—even for the bus, even for Hamilton.

I beat it down the steps of the bus, push through the glass doors again. I think about recording the number of the bus to make a complaint. But I doubt that'll have any effect. I sprint home instead to call a cab. There's no way I want this driver taking me anywhere tonight. I'll be late for work, but I can sort that out later. My supervisor will have to believe this story—no way I could ever make this up.

NO LOITERING

SWEATING

Matt Hern

CHICAGO, JULY 2002

The bus is old and slow, and the heat makes everything liquid. People get on and get off. The bus moves forward but doesn't get anywhere. We've been in Pilsen forever. I've read the same story about the Sox game for the last hour. I slip back into a daze, stare at the bricks going by and then return to the story, still surprised at Frank Thomas's continuing fall from grace. What the hell happened to that guy?

I'm coming from the South Side heading up to Pedro Albizu Campos High School to visit a friend and to check the place out. My Vancouver nerves and brain are still adjusting to the temperature after a couple of days in the city. I have taken to carrying around a full-size bath towel to mop up the sweat that comes pouring from my face and head all day. I walk around the city looking like I just got out of the shower.

Everyone on the bus is Mexican except me. At a stop I watch a guy selling watermelons from the back of his truck. I wonder if I could get out, buy a melon, and get back on again before the bus leaves. Probably. I would break the melon in half over my knee, give one half to someone else, and put my whole face inside my half. As this plan is forming I watch a young man, maybe nineteen or twenty years old stagger up the steps, half-walking, half-falling.

The kid is pretty sincerely disabled. He has a full-body affliction like cerebral palsy or something that keeps his limbs and mouth and tongue and face mostly out of his control. His knees are bent in on each other so that his lower legs angle towards the ground at forty-five degrees and he is forced to balance on the inside edges of his feet, barely staying upright. His arms are bent tight at the elbow and lie across his body, wrists and hands flapping under his chin. His tongue hangs half out of his mouth which gapes open and shut, gulping for air as drool trickles down one side of his chin.

It is clear that despite his disability he's pretty capable. It's a major production getting his money out of his pocket: tottering at the edge of the stairwell as the bus pulls out, manoeuvering his hand into his pocket, pulling out the right change, getting it into the receptacle. It's no joke, but he pulls it off. He has tidy, clean clothes on, his hair has obviously just been washed and gelled, his eyes are big and alert. It is clear that this guy is on an excursion and he is excited to be out. More than that, he is thrilled, exuberant. He is in a great mood, and his joy is palpable. He smiles hugely, tries extravagantly to make eye contact with everyone on the bus, words come pouring out of his mouth—loud, eager, incomprehensible.

This guy is dripping charisma, and he is more than ready to make friends with someone, anyone. Still, I resist meeting his gaze in my self-conscious, Waspy, Canadian way. I definitely want to check the man out, he is begging for closer inspection, but I am reluctant to make him a spectacle. Actually, it's more because I'm afraid of the direct interaction. If I look at the dude, maybe I'll have to talk to him or he'll sit with me or he'll drool on me or something. I hate this tendency as much as anyone though, so I make an effort to smile openly at him, all the while dreading that he will sit next to me. Maybe it's not a Canadian thing because everyone on the bus is doing the same. All looking, trying not to look, resisting him.

The little girl behind me whispers to her mom, "Is he a retard?"

"Si," she answers, and pushes the girl's pointing finger back down to her lap.

The kid doesn't mind being a spectacle at all, however. In fact that's what he is attempting. No one is making him uneasy. He is trying to get people to look at him. It is pretty evident that he is completely aware of his blatant otherness, and he doesn't care. He just bombs through that shit with personality.

The kid never stops talking, way loud, and when it is clear that no one is going to invite him to sit down beside them, he staggers up and down the bus, visiting with everyone, admiring their clothes, grabbing their hands, laughing maniacally, showing them his ID: Marvin Harris. I try hard to understand what he's saying when he collapses in the seat next to mine because it is certain that he is saying *something*, it's not just gibberish. I think he is going up to Milwaukee Avenue to buy some cologne—maybe. I am kind of distracted by the way Marv holds my hand, stroking it and holding it unsettlingly near his crotch.

After a couple of minutes of us conversing, the bus pulls over sharply and another person gets on. It is a startlingly beautiful man. He is big and seriously muscular, but not in a cheesy way. He looks like he is carved out of marble, coffee-black skin, razor-sharp goatee, and g-funked out with a very manicured style. His do-rag is crisp and perfectly tied. His profligate ice is tasteful, his Air Jordans immaculate, his Nike ankle socks whiter than white, matching his T-shirt with presslines like they were drawn on with a ruler. He sits in the front side seats, the ones meant for old people. Maybe to give everyone a clear view.

There is no ambiguity with this guy. He is simply beautiful—he knows it, he knows that everyone else around him knows it. He has an impenetrable arrogance, a tangible aloofness, a regal can't-touch-this thing around him that is impossible to miss. Everyone on the bus, of course, stares long and hard. The gangsta looks at no one. He stares off, allowing people to ogle extensively, but discreetly.

Marvin, however, is not discreet. Like everyone else there he obviously finds the gansta totally attractive. Unlike the rest of us though, he has no hesitation in doing what we all want to do but would never dream of. He leaps to his feet, stumbles up to man, collapses down beside him, and immediately starts touching. He does exactly what I would have done—he slides right up close and starts stroking the gangsta's thigh. G's thigh is huge, defined, and hairless. His jean shorts have slid up a little and there is about four inches of black skin that the kid starts fondling, gazing adoringly at G-funk's face, drool flowing freely.

The gansta twitches sharply, spins disdainfully, pushes the kid back a little and says loudly, "What the fuck you think you're doing, man? Get yer goddam hands off me!"

The kid loves this. He makes a long moaning kind of sound, smiles hugely, rips off a few lines and cuddles back up. This time he goes for the gold and jabs his hand right in the man's crotch. The gangsta jumps up, flinging Marv aside, "Jesus, homes. Quit that shit." And he moves right across the aisle to the opposite side seats.

It's hardly like this is going to dissuade the kid. He immediately follows the beautiful man, sits down beside him again, scooping up a hand with both of his, stroking it and admiring the rings. Until now I have been completely delighted with the whole situation. It's genius. But now, I'm feeling a little worried for Marvin. If he doesn't quit, how long will it be before this huge homophobe just drills him? It wouldn't be wholly unjustified. There are mitigating circumstances—the kid's disability and the gansta's beauty—but still, it's pretty overt sexual harassment.

Amazingly to me though, the beautiful man leans away and looks down sneeringly, but doesn't pull his hand away. G-funk relaxes a little and allows the kid to hold and caress his hand. Maybe he's cutting his losses, realizing that he is just going to have to suffer this kid until his stop and hand-holding is as good as it's going to get. Marv is delighted, throws his arms around the man's neck, and kisses his cheek. Again the man leans away, pushes the kid back a little, and says, "Sheeeit," but that's it. He stays in place.

The two of them sit there like teenagers, hand in hand, until the kid can't stand it any more. He reaches between the gangsta's legs with a pleading look. The man grabs his wrist, rejects it, and says, "Alright, that's it. You just got yerself cut off, man. Go sit over there." He points across the aisle to the seats they had started in. Marvin's head drops. He realizes he's blown it and he's crushed. He lingers, hoping the edict will be rescinded, but the gangsta isn't having it. In a deep and authoritative voice, he says, "Now, dude. Get over there. Now!" And gives him a little shove.

Marv is devastated. He was perfectly happy and now he's exiled. He tries big, wet eyes, he tries to stay, but the man looks away out the window. The kid slinks over to his seat, tail between his legs. His disappointment and heartbreak fill the bus, they press on my chest, my throat. He collapses on his seat, crying big tears, not loudly, gulping for air. He drives his hand through his hair repeatedly, Tourettically, and makes a mess of it. All his joyful exuberance is destroyed and he is perfectly, completely sad. The scope of the tragedy is almost too much.

The beautiful man won't relent though. He won't even look at the kid. And it's hard to blame him. He wasn't really mean or anything. I have no idea what I would have done. With a sudden twitch the gangsta pulls the bell, and says sharply to the driver, "Here, man. Lemme out." He's had enough and is going to make a break for it.

Marvin's head snaps up and watches the man stride past. The gansta stops and holds on, swaying gently as the bus slows against the curb, his triceps bulging. The doors open and the gansta takes one step down, pauses, shakes his head, and sighs extravagantly. His hands drop to his side in child-like resignation as he turns back. "Ahhh, shit, man." He makes a rapper hand gesture. "Let's go." The kid looks up in disbelief. "Yeah, I'm talking to you, homeslice. Let's go!

C'mon . . . *C'mon*, negro!" It almost seems like he smiles as he jumps out of the bus, but really it was more like a grimace.

It's like the sun came out after a whole winter of rain. Marvin leaps up, an indeterminate noise bellowing from him and falls over himself trying to get out of the bus fast enough. As we pull away, I can see him staggering after the beautiful gansta trying to catch up, reaching for his hand.

OUTSIDE-IN

Marc Boudignon

There is a drunk kid to my right—and I've never seen this before—mock-humping the picture of a lingerie model on the streetcar shelter. I have my arms wrapped around my torso, head hooded and hanging over the crumbling edge of the curb like a lamp post trying to illuminate the position of the streetcar ahead from the other pacing vehicles: cars, bikes, mopeds, the odd skateboard. As a couple in a rickshaw pass—she holding a rose—the throng of fashionable revellers I'm beside explodes in cheers (or jeers, it's hard to tell). A few of them even hold up bottles prolonging a toast that should have ended hours ago. I check my cell phone for the time. There's still half an hour until the drinks cease for good tonight, but a large yawn steals my lofty aspirations and reminds me that a pleasant dream needs me more.

The three eyes of the streetcar blink in between the last few cars on its way to our stop, the home stretch. As it slows, the wheels make their deafening scream along the rusted tracks, and only I brace my ears to muffle the intrusion. The driver misjudges his distance, jolting forward toward the group's huddle. As he does so, a blue spark explodes from the contact wire, attracting the attention of no one because everyone here is too patient or drunk to care.

The halloo of a burgeoning thundershower has our social city gather quickly at the foot of the slowing streetcar. The headlights and the saffron glow of the fluorescent interior, a beacon of dry refuge, glints in our eyes, and we shuffle to it like moths toward a patio lantern. We, the last animals on Noah's Ark, are outrunning the bellowing sound of our extinction, and all of it converges at this moment.

The streetcar comes to a total halt, and the double doors collapse back like partition walls revealing the warmth, the dirt, and the driver in full. He does not greet us, but simply extends his hand gripping a booklet of free passes to keep going. Ignoring him, I move through the row of mostly empty seats, realizing the existential suspicion that we're all alone in our travels, and so for that I choose a single seat beside the window with the heater on the left side.

This streetcar—perhaps in particular—is full of diversion. For one, there is a glass bottle that began its journey from the seniors' seat up front when I arrived, rolling from side to side, zigzagging its way to the teenagers in the back. There are a couple of passengers, like me, who are tracking its progress; the bottle travels in curves, moving in an organized dance step of semicircles, rattling its way to the finish. Its dance is not a graceful one, however, and it seems as though every third step involves a slam into the side of the wall; the act of the glass hitting the moulded plastic of the streetcar flooring makes an obtrusive clink-clank each time, but is neither frequent, nor annoying, enough to warrant anyone doing anything about it. On its fifth rotation, the bottle, with its colourfully expressive strawberry-kiwi outfit, eventually fulfills its destiny, reaching the other end, and head butts an unwitting teenager's shoe. The Air Jordan—as clean as the floor of the streetcar is not—kicks the bottle in retaliation and sends it jitterbugging back up the length of the streetcar from where it began. After the following stop, the driver accelerates, forcing us all to jerk backwards, and this prompts the bottle's dance down the aisle again for us to watch.

In the meantime, the rain has started outside and drops have dotted the large windowpane my elbow is pressed against. My head feels heavy from a workplace filled with recycled air and this city of smoke, so my hand props it up, making me appear more pensive than I really am. My thoughts dally, formulating into loose connections on the way to no point until a cold feeling draws me back here. I lift my elbow and see that it has been dipping into a growing pool of tar-black water streaming down from the roof of the streetcar. My jacket is soaked, and the wet works through the cotton fibres, up my arm as if it was a disease, until it inevitably touches my skin; I need to shed these layers. Seeping through the invisible holes around us, the water starts to fill up the floor and makes the inside sweat. Lines of rain swish with the vehicle's every punch and shutter along the corduroy aisle, and the passengers (the sober ones) lift their feet as the waves splash past them. Mr. Air Jordan smartly puts his shoes up on the seat. Everyone begins to creep away from the walls, cowering from their contact points. I take my bag and place it on my lap, fearful for my papers and my wallet inside. One person recoils from her plush seat that has suddenly become infused with liquid, now transferred to the back pockets of her jeans; she chooses not to sit down again. We all feel the outside coming in on us, and the damp street odour this streetcar forever contains is duly released, permeating our unprotected air, gassing us into submission.

One of the drunks—the guy sitting beside the one who had the poster girl—complains about the smell ("Who pissed in here?! No, really, who pissed in the streetcar?") and decides that he'll rectify it by opening the window. This brings in the rain even more, and the acid shrapnel pelts the arm of his leather jacket like machine gun fire. Now there are other sounds, too. The whole orchestra of the city streams in with its bleating horns and temper-tantrum sirens, the avalanche pounding of garbage trucks, and the dissident howl of casual anger. The rain has done its job on the pavement, pushing its embedded oils to the surface, changing the texture of the noise. Every car that passes within earshot makes a sound like tearing paper as they part the waters at the base of their wheels. The more I focus on it, the less I can bear its violence and frequency. Still, there are even worse sounds—the streetcar opposite us is making a turn, and the wheels scrape the tracks like a file sharpening a knife. All the dull edges are honed.

There is a blanket flash, and for a moment I'm unsure whether or not it's the streetcar or nature that produced it. People notice it, and a beat later, the lights go out around us—the reflection on the metal goes dead and the advertisements no longer pulse with product rainbows. The transient inhabitants are silent. Another beat and the lights return, the ruckus swells to normality, yet the streetcar itself remains dormant. We are now not going anywhere, which is nowhere closer to my bed and my real refuge. The driver's voice on the PA system, searing like air from a blow dryer into my ear, tells us "Wemightbeafewminutes." He hurries his words through the pops and fizzles of the speakers as if he was being charged long distance to the back of the streetcar.

Most people wait patiently; the drunks stay cemented in their seats because they've had it with the whole balance thing; a lone man walks to the front, silently collects his transfer, and after disembarking, plods ahead for a more worthy vessel. I deliberate my own options to stay or go, and after a few moments thinking—the street, the drunks, the bottle, the cell phones all circling around me—I realize I'll be alone in my wending home, and that my quiet wants are my own. Sometimes, I figure it's best to make one's own way through the city, so I step down and pass through the accordion double doors, jumping into the pool. I look back at the streetcar as it closes itself to me, and I see it as it actually is now: a grounded monument, nothing in a world full of speeding things. It sits statically in the middle of rhythm, and like water, the other vehicles find ways of overtaking it, carrying on around it. Standing here, waiting to go at the green, I want to be like the cars, the people, the sound, and the light—in motion, constantly, until I am forced to rest.

TO MONTREAL, BY BUS, FOR THE GAME

matt robinson

there was the moment: racked
long and rigid, extended all slow-frame cinematic between

the widening eyes' competing vices, stretched rubberband's
near-limit taut, of the rain. all of—a sea now

un-parted after years—a sudden. the instant biblical,
or near. the sky a headlong torrent tear; like

what we imagine must be the theatrical
interior of a drain just after a plug's grudging acquiescence; a

science of singular purpose, direction. (this is what proximity does
to proportion: explodes it—

our fractions and our counting—beyond any
reasonable mathematics.) and our telling? we hadn't yet been

drinking, so when the highway uncurtained, stepped out of
the rain, smoothed the now drying lines

of its travel suit's legs to their former slick grey fabric weave
again, we simply turned walkmans up one notch

further, turned away from both the streaking
windows and each other, dove into the crisp assurance of our

magazines and papers, drowning out the possibility
of conversation; tried to deafen the crashing and thrum of

the water in our ears. wished we could roll down the windows
and drink the air: gulp it loud until it

parched, until it cracked the hollow gulleys of our throats down
to our lungs. left us spilt, and split.

Suspect Baggage

Allen Moore

Frankfurt, Germany
May 4, 1992, Monday Evening

9:11 PM

Earlier this afternoon, my flight home to Vancouver was delayed by ten hours, with the revised departure set for eleven-thirty this evening. If the delay is extended by another half hour, there will not be a flight. At midnight, Frankfurt's airport will close. I don't know when it will reopen. Public sector workers in Germany have begun rotating strikes, shutting down facilities for days at a time, and this airport is their next target. Several hours ago, the roar of thousands of passengers, flight announcements, and aircraft engines filled the bright, sunlit complex. But as the day turned to night, the airport became quiet, vacant, and sterile.

The passengers of my flight recognize one another now. When we were told of the delay, we were offered an afternoon cruise along the Rhine. So off we went for a day on the water. We even had our own boat. As we sailed along the river under the warm skies of spring, surrounded by vineyards and castles, we connected. Of course, the booze helped. The afternoon was worth the delay. Others may disagree.

9:15 PM

A few dozen of us burn time in the Leonardo da Vinci Lounge, somewhere in the labyrinth of Frankfurt's airport.

"Bella, honey," a man pleads at a nearby table, "I think you've had enough to drink." Bella snatches the glass of white wine from the table and spills a little on her blue blouse. Her two preschool daughters play with their food, flinging small nuggets onto the floor when their parents are not watching.

"It's wine," Bella explains to her husband, "it doesn't count." She drains half the glass in one mischievous gulp.

Most of the people in the lounge sit in solitude; several write. The airport is quiet—too quiet. People frequently check the time. I am not the only one wondering what may happen at midnight. Or what may *not* happen.

9:21 PM

"Shhurrrrre," Bella says to the waiter when offered a second glass of wine (which probably doesn't count). "Why not? Hey! Get it? Wine ought!" She winks at the young man then gives her husband a sly smile as if she were posing for da Vinci. Bella's older daughter pours Coca-Cola over a sandwich. The bread turns dark as it soaks up the fluid. The child continues to pour the drink, filling the plate to its rim.

I feel lucky to be single.

9:33 PM

Two men discuss history, airplanes, and art. They drink beer. The big man weaves his black beard with his fingers, stopping at times to push his thick glasses up the ridge of his nose. His dark grey suit gives him the air of academic authority. His running shoes do not. He explains that Mr. da Vinci failed to complete his studies of flight because "He was a homosexual and became infatuated with David, whom he later carved up." I cannot decipher whether David was the victim of a fifteenth-century crime and wound up in pieces, or if the crime sits closer to home (closer to Frankfurt at least) and Michelangelo has been slighted. Clues may follow.

The professor finishes all major subjects with a few words of what he claims to be Latin. "Conundrum absurdus equilibrium" (or something) he says, scrutinizing Bella as she bails with the brats. His baritone voice draws attention and people turn to find him struggling to separate his beard from his wrist watch. "Cheeses Murphy," I think he says, possibly identifying a clump in his wiry mat.

When I'm tired and grouchy, I paint my peers with an acid brush. And wine ought?

9:38 PM

Dinner arrives, paid for by the airline. Eight years ago, I had a multi-hour delay at Toronto's Pearson Airport. After a lengthy debate with an airline representative, I was finally granted remuneration for a single slice of pizza. More calories had been consumed pleading the case. Toronto, Onterrible.

9:51 PM

The waiter approaches the table formerly occupied by Bella and her beastly brats. Armed with a cloth, the young man pauses as if trying to interpret the message expressed by the soggy food and the plate filled to its rim with Coca-Cola. The message is this: Forget the cloth, you need a Shop Vac.

10:16 PM

Having dined and disgraced da Vinci's place, we the weary, and in some cases wasted, drift toward gate B-34, wondering if there is an airplane outside. There is! Passengers in rumpled clothing fill the waiting area. In the hallway outside the gate's lounge, huge Zamboni-like floor-sweeping machines glide over the acres of floor space and erase our path, the evening's final migration. The rest of the airport is empty.

10:19 PM

A young woman carrying an infant stands at the window and stares into the night toward the distant flickering lights of Frankfurt. She holds her child close, the focus of all her reserve. In this crowd, she not only looks the most tired, but also the most dignified.

10:23 PM

"Impendium exodus maximus" or something. It's the professor in running shoes again. People roll their eyes when the air reverberates with yet another piece of nonsensicus intellectium blurbus. I hope he keeps it up.

10:26 PM

We smell like farm animals. Perspiration and sauerkraut reaching critical mass. Sound reason to fear the aircraft cabin.

10:55 PM

On board! I'm in seat 27A beside a window. So far, no takers for 27B. What if Murphy's Law drops a large odorous gorilla into that seat? I contemplate the claustrophobic hell of sitting next to someone the size of N people (where N is large), overfilling 27B and spilling excess corpulence into 27A.

11:01 PM

Fear glands secrete, for I see that a large hairy beast with damp armpits has found his way out of the zoo and onto this airplane. And he is coming down the aisle!

11:03 PM

Murphy put the Cro-Magnon half a dozen rows ahead. But I wasn't entirely forgotten—behind me in row 28 colons override colognes. I'm going to see if the oxygen mask works.

11:05 PM

An elderly lady from Germany, now living in Canada, takes the seat next to me. Phew, what a relief! She is friendly and seems happy with her seat. I wonder if we had similar fears. I don't ask.

11:06 PM

Chaos in the aisles. People jam their stuff into the overhead compartments. Short tempers, grey faces, and black-bagged eyes. The young mother with the infant moves slowly down the aisle carrying a large bag over her shoulder. She squeezes past the great girth of the Cro-Magnon, who rummages through a bag in the overhead. A baby bottle drops from the mother's bag. Cro-Magnon looks down, sees the bottle on the floor, ignores it, and resumes digging through his bag. The mother stops and stares blank-faced toward the rear of the cabin. An older gent reaches for the bottle and slides it into the mother's bag.

11:15 PM

"Are you a student?" my seatmate asks me as I write about her asking me if I am a student.

Sure, a student of law (Murphy's), human behaviour (drunken), anthropology (Cro-Magnon), and Latin (bastardized).

11:16 PM

Two languages dominate the cabin banter: English and German. Over top of this, two languages rattle off various preflight announcements: English and *French*. Hint: This is a Canadian airline. The Canadians smile; the Germans don't get it.

11:17 PM

The captain gets on the intercom: "Please get seated as soon as possible everyone." He reiterates what we already know: The aircraft must be off the ground before midnight, before strike action closes the airfield. What language will make these people sit?

11:19 PM

"You're very busy writing about something," my neighbour informs me. She is most friendly. "What a commotion this is," she adds, agreeing closely with what I am writing about. "What are you writing about?" she asks.

11:21 PM

"If there is a doctor on board, please approach one of the attendants." That one made it in English and German. Bureaucracy overruled. The crew attend to a woman a dozen rows ahead. She is in tears.

11:25 PM

"We have a security problem," the captain says. "There is a piece of suspect baggage on board." He explains that the ground crew will have to reopen the cargo hold and remove the item.

"Oh, dear," the lady next to me says, "what next I wonder?"

11:27 PM

The cabin is noticeably quieter now. After all the chaotic shuffling, a few simple words brought remarkable order. "Security problem." "Suspect baggage." Many tired eyes have opened wide.

11:47 PM

The ground crew has removed a lot of cargo and their work continues at a hurried pace. *Bang! Thump!* The movements below shake the whole airplane. This is a DC-10, boys, go easy on her. They've probably been asked to remove everything and close the hatch. We haven't time to sift for suspect baggage. *Pull it all and we'll explain things to the passengers as we fly through the cold, black night.*

11:51 PM

The captain states that an ambulance crew will board the aircraft to assist someone. He asks everyone to remain seated. No roaming the cabin. "Everything is fine and we will be off the ground very shortly." Everything does not feel fine.

11:54 PM

Paramedics arrive, their bright yellow jackets radiating authority. Two carry the sick woman off the aircraft using a stretcher. A few others open up the overhead compartments in the area where she had been sitting. They search for unclaimed baggage. "Can someone identify this bag? Yes? It is yours? Good. And this one? Okay. And this?" They work fast, slamming the compartments closed as they move down the aisle. The passengers watch closely and sit quietly still.

11:56 PM

A man sitting a few rows ahead springs to his feet, grabs his bag, and storms up the aisle. "I wish to get out," he says, "enough is enough." In the wake of his departure, the paramedics expand their search. They work along both aisles now.

At what point does the herd instinct take over and drive everyone from their seats? Surely we are on the cusp of a mass exodus. The tension in the air is enough to carry three hundred tonnes. A tightrope spans the Atlantic. Everyone is silent. Our shared concern makes us look a little more alike.

MIDNIGHT

Sitting. Waiting. Hoping.

12:05 AM

A deep hum fills the cabin as engine number one spools up. The tow vehicle moves the aircraft away from the gate, away from our cargo, and away from the suspect baggage.

Somewhere in the rows behind me a baby fires up. Scream all you want, kid, but you're coming with us.

12:07 AM

"They are being quite thorough," my neighbour in 27B says. Indeed, the preflight explanation of the safety vest and emergency procedures seems painstakingly comprehensive. Stimulated passengers pay close attention.

Bella nods off.

12:09 AM

This evening's din, a chorus of sorts, features three engines and two babies. So far, no percussion.

12:14 AM

We are off the ground! The aircraft burns two tonnes of fuel per hour to produce 140,000 pounds of thrust, and yet the roar is no match for two shrieking infants.

1:31 AM

The likelihood of our having a bomb on board is infinitesimal, almost non-existent, yet something lingers. Everyone is spooked. A phantom rides with us and draws presence from our fear. It is trapped aboard the aircraft, just as we are, unable to leave until we do. The infants shriek, but this is not what keeps us awake.

Move to the Back

Chris LaVigne

"Move to the back!" hollers the bus driver and I know he's not talking to me. Hearing the order, the mass of standing passengers collectively shrug and domino their eyes toward the rear, waiting for someone else to move first. The succession of glances stops abruptly as a woman turns and hits a newspaper wall, beyond which lies an uninterested man's face and metres of unoccupied bus floor. Feeling responsible for the bus driver's command, the woman tries her best passive-aggressive stare, but it has no effect. The man remains motionless, as does the throng awaiting his movement.

From outside, dejected sighs and irate curses filter in through the closing doors of the bus as murmurs of disapproval pass down the line of standing passengers and are met only by the casual sound of a newspaper's pages being turned.

"Health Care System In Decline" hollers a headline from the front page, which I can barely read from my hard-fought seat at the back of the bus. I'm sitting on one of the seats that face sideways meaning I have to spend the entire ride pretending not to look at people even though they're in my direct line of view. I've already exhausted reading all of the advertisements and I hate looking at my feet, so I cautiously allow my gaze to roam, avoiding eye contact with a well-practised precision. I wish that the newspaper man had moved back like he should have, because then I'd be able to see more than the headlines.

I stretch my legs out into the empty aisle. Down at the front of the bus, three or four people are probably tightroping the little red safety line and praying the bus driver finds no reason to show off his occupation's penchant for sudden braking. The passive-aggressive woman is shaking her head in a new, but equally futile, attempt at alerting the newspaper man of his missing guilt. Behind her, six people are sardined into a space the size of an entry-level office cubicle. Their grumbled rage is muted by the rumbling of the bus as it lumbers onward in search of more passengers.

Soon, the bus stops again. Uncirculated air becomes charged with motionless anger. Finally, one of the six sardines has had enough and explodes, "For Christ's sake, move to the back!" The newspaper man, his eyes never leaving their reading material, merely compresses himself against the seat closest to him. His movement, however slight, is still enough to uncork the mass behind him and they burst toward the rear of the bus. I have to draw my feet underneath my seat for fear of being trampled on. Only a couple of people make it to the back, though, as some of the others refuse to go any further than the rear doors. Fresh sardines begin loading the bus and although everyone gets on board this time, they're packed even tighter than they were before.

Flanked by his new allies, the newspaper man turns another page and continues to ignore the crowd. "African Poverty Aid In Disarray" a headline announces. The front doors swish closed.

One of the lucky people to have made it to the back is now standing in front of me adding his crotch to my available views. I'm debating whether it would be better or worse if he turned around.

We're still not moving yet. The driver is presumably waiting for a break in traffic when I see a person running for the bus. I hear her footsteps stomp past, but moments later I feel the bus lurching into motion without having heard the doors open and close. I swivel around as the bus pulls away to see the woman standing on the curb, slumped over and muttering curses upon the race of bus drivers.

I always get a strange thrill from seeing people miss their bus. It has something to do with the glass and the distance that separates me from them. I feel safe to revel in their misery with little chance of their seeing the smile that grows on my face as the bus leaves them behind. One time, a man had the poor luck to not only miss the bus, but to be drenched as the bus tires spun through a puddle. Rarely do you ever see strangers so embarrassingly close to tears, and yet all I could do was poke my friend in the ribs so that together we could point and laugh.

I rotate my head back around to find that my standing neighbour has himself rotated, answering my question by proving that his crotch was indeed the lesser of two evils. In a panic, I swerve my eyes to the floor where shoes and feet offer less potential for undesirable mental images. I wish I had a book, or one of those cell phones with a video game, or anything to distract me from my surroundings.

Boredom and curiosity turn my attention to the front of the bus again where the sardines are forced to sniff each other's shampoos and deodorants, dodge swinging backpacks, and snuggle together like lovers in a Hollywood close-up. The newspaper man indifferently flips another page, creases his paper, and turns it around. A picture of Rosa Parks makes eye contact with me, but I can't make out the headline.

The bus slows down and jerks over to the side of the road. There's a stir from the front as one of the passengers attempts to make his way to the rear doors to disembark. It's not an easy task as his path is blocked by a dense, uncompromising mass of humanity. His struggle reminds me of a salmon swimming against the current to its spawning ground. Or Moses faced with the immensity of the Red Sea. Only this poor soul has neither instinct nor divine intervention on his side. He can rely on only himself.

At the stop, two people are waiting to get on the bus and they both board quickly. There's some commotion as one of them has some trouble with her transfer. The disembarking man is still several rows away from freedom. He shoves people aside in desperation. He stumbles, spins, and swears his way toward the doors. Scowls and shaking heads trail behind him from people with stepped-on feet.

The man is two metres from the doors, breaking through the newspaper man's flanks like a running back through a squad of linebackers. I observe him the way commuters survey the aftermath of a traffic accident. The man's arm scythes through the air to reach for the bar that triggers the opening of the doors. As he does so, his elbow catches the newspaper and rips it out of newspaper man's hands. The man's fingers finally wrap around the bar, but at the same moment the bus engine begins to rumble. The man shakes the bar back and forth, but nothing happens. The doors do not open.

The man's eyes cloud over with tears. He utters a noise made of equal parts exhaustion and rage. His shoulders sink in defeat. Passengers look to the floor and the ceiling to avoid being implicated in his helplessness. Briefly, the man peers toward the front of the bus where, beyond the sardines, the bus driver sits oblivious. Now fully without hope, the man leans back against a pole and waits for the next stop.

I turn to the newspaper man who looks wholly amused by the other man's predicament. Grinning, he retrieves his reading matter and flattens it back into a readable shape. The headline I can see tells me that the government thinks too many people are on welfare.

Before he starts reading, the newspaper man looks around the bus for the first time. Our eyes meet and I realize that the smile on his face matches the one that has grown on mine. Using his eyebrows, he indicates the other man, slouched over in defeat, and then shakes his head. His eyes widen and his lips purse in an expression of condemnation, as though he had nothing but scorn for the entire human race. It feels like I'm looking into a mirror.

I turn to the other man, fragile and pathetic. I turn back to the newspaper man who has again erected his paper shield. Finally, I turn and pin my eyes to the floor, wishing only that I had something to keep me distracted from all of this.

Memory, the Night Streetcar, Toronto

Kevin Irie

11:30 p.m. The College streetcar heads out, west from downtown Toronto, night ride home, after the movies, just before curfew. Young couples sitting side by side.

At Queen's Park, boarding, come legions of mothers up from Bay Street. Their work shift over, cleaning the offices. Their voices pitched against the silence of teens who recognize their parents approaching. Mothers whose sons and daughters ride home. The streetcar suddenly becomes the neighbourhood street lit up for inspection, a church interior at late-night mass, each seat a pew where so-and-so's son and so-and-so's daughter share their communal despair together. The smiles and whispers of mothers staring. No wonder bourgeois suburban life seems exotic for such offspring:

mothers always home at midnight, neighbours safe behind picture windows, fathers rich enough to doze in their dens.

Here, parents and progeny disembark together, the mothers behind their young like a procession marching past families on porches, in darkness. Or judgement. *Banish the porch*, some budding architect notes in his mind. *Let him get his licence*, a daughter prays. Vows of various kinds are sworn in secret, awaiting future delivery. The streetcar heading further into the night, freedom a passenger with neither a curfew nor neighbour who knows it by name.

WELCOME TO YOU
FOR YOUR VISIT

Cool

Stephen Johnson

Damon and I pull down the brims of our cheap fedoras, and leap into the subway car. Train doors close behind us in a massive swoosh. No turning back. We snap three times—*snap snap snap*—and look around. Packed house. Morning commute. Not much room to move. The sounds of private thoughts and newspapers. Damon and I look at each other, get into the crouch, and begin to hum our song for the day, "Cool," from the musical, *West Side Story*: "Da-dum, da-dum, dum da dum dum . . ."

It's 1992, the Berlin Wall has fallen, and dour East German businessmen and women look up from their laps. Sidelong glances and sneers.

"Boy, boy, crazy boy. Get cool, boy . . ." We break off; Damon snakes down one aisle, I jostle down the other way. The passengers coming from the grey East to the shiny, shiny West seem a little stunned by it all. No one wants to be caught watching. So we jump into the void. "Got a rocket in your pocket. Keep coolly cool, boy!"

We fly down the aisles, all snaps and big smiles, a couple of cool guys from California, USA, who just met a few weeks ago, who are living in an apartment abandoned by East Berliners fleeing to the West. We're living in a squat with other misfits, bohemians, travellers, artists, and criminals from all over the world. We're trying to make a few Deutschmarks so we can eat and drink today.

Snap snap snap. We shimmy our hats. "Eine kleine spende, just a little change. Danke." By the end of this three-hour shift, we'll have said "danke" about five hundred times.

We're starting to turn a few heads. Damon's charming a young mother with two children, stooping to sing, and they're laughing. Beautiful, yes, this is a good train . . . go to her with the hat . . . don't tarry, D., work your way down the car, D. I work toward the front so when it stops, we can finish, collect our money, and move on. Remember the supreme law of busking: Get people to look into your eyes, and they're yours.

Snap snap snap. East Berliners are leaving behind everything but clothes and memories. The mother and her daughters, a scowling old man shaking his head, refusing to look up at me, a sulky teen wearing an Iron Maiden T-shirt.

What can we *give* you? New televisions? Apartments in the West? Freedom? Think of us as a kind of welcoming committee. We will mend your broken borders with song. Give you a Marshall Plan of Music.

"Yeah! Crazy! Cool!" Now people are actually *smiling*. The girls love us, the guys in suits are still not sure. Just keep singing. The buildings outside from East to West: grey becomes green, tunnels become bridges, Alexanderplatz turns into a mall.

A group of teenage girls at the end of the car is craning over at the commotion. I can't let them go. I get into the crouch and slink over. They're giggling, probably laughing at us. I go to one knee, doff my hat, and they give me one mark. That's all right. The old woman next to them gives me a five-mark piece.

The train begins its brake-whine, the slow down, the passenger-purge. I look frantically for Damon—we gotta wrap up this song, finish up the chit-chat, hit the hat, dump the change into our pockets, and jump to the platform, to the next train at the next station.

We make eye contact and rush out the doors. We're barely going to make it. Let's go, D. We scramble to the next car to begin the song again, and again, and again on our perfect run.

I look back, and want to run down the aisle one last time and do a big slide on my knees. A finale. A flourish.

As Damon and I get jammed up in the bustle of people between cars, I figure we're either ambassadors of the dream, the pleasure-promise of the West, or we might be its nightmare. Or maybe we're just young. We don't admit the greyness and hardness of the times, but for a few moments, neither did the riders of those trains.

We break free of the bustle between trains, slip inside the closing doors of the new car, pull at the brims of our fedoras, and get into the crouch—*snap snap snap*.

Barranca del Cobre

Jeremiah Aherne

Mike and I were on the Chihuahua-Pacifico railroad, late January, headed east from Los Mochis on the Gulf of California up into the Sierra Madre Occidental to see the *Barranca del Cobre*, the Copper Canyon. Five times wider and one-and-a-half times deeper than the Grand Canyon in the good ol' U.S.of A. Barranca del Cobre was going to be a big change from the sunny beaches of the Baja Peninsula where we had been trying to learn to surf since before Christmas—two Prairie boys thrashing away in the ocean.

Kenny was one of the English-speaking people who we met on the ferry from La Paz on the Baja over to the mainland. He was second-generation Japanese hailing from San Francisco and the only Asian we had seen in Mexico—a phenomenon heightened by the swarms of Mexican children who followed him everywhere pointing and shouting, "*Cheena. Cheena.*" Chinese. I don't know which annoyed him more, the children crowding around and screaming at him or the fact that they thought he was Chinese and not Japanese. Kenny was a little uptight. It was he who approached Mike and I as possible escorts for his hike over the Continental Divide, right through the meat of the Copper Canyon. As he described the first part of the journey, a bus ride from Divisadero down to the bottom of the canyon, it took all of two seconds for us to say, "Hell, yeah."

Also amongst the budget travellers who had congregated on the same part of the ferry deck, a seemingly designated holding ground for the non-Mexicans, were three of the pastiest young Englishwomen I've ever laid eyes on. They wore hats the size of beach umbrellas and slathered on infant-grade sunblock every ten minutes—and this was while staying adamantly in the shade. They all looked like Katharine Hepburn in *The African Queen* and they carried around weighty, canonical books at all times. On the flip-side there was the couple from New Zealand, Kiwi accents thick as sap, who were Southern-Hemisphere-no-ozone darker than any of the Mexicans.

As always seems to happen when foreigners meet in a foreign place, it was these same people from the ferry that piled onto the train car with us the next morning. The Chihuahua-Pacifico railroad was completed in 1961, a vicious project that sliced and blasted its way through the formidable mountains, overcoming all logical impasses with thirty-nine bridges and eighty-six tunnels. We were on the first-class train, which meant that there were seats and the windows opened. The trip was stunning; it was an awe-inspiring mixture of rugged natural beauty and man's loftiest endeavours. The bridges spanned chasms thousands of feet deep, white-water rivers thread-like at the bottom, birds flying high above the river still far below the tracks. The tunnels went on for miles.

There was one heartbreaking aspect to this spectacular train ride and it wasn't the hard seats or the stinky heat of the cars. The locals, not tourists, for whom this train trip seemed to be the only form of public transport to get them from the Gulf to the interior, used the open windows as garbage portals. Mexican families, who had brought their food and drinks for the day, would casually toss the empty cans, bottles, and chip bags out the window. That this had been going on unabated for years was evident in the yard sale of junk littered along the tracks. At one point, I saw a mother bundle up the remains of her family's packed lunch in a garbage bag and heave it out the window and watch contentedly as it fell—for a good minute—into the gorge below.

The next morning was cold, not ocean-breeze-Mexico cold but real, almost Canadian cold and there was snow and ice crouched against the north sides of the surrounding buildings. The bus sat idling in the *zocalo* and the sun hadn't yet made it over the red-clay-tiled roofs; the exhaust, like our breath, hung in the growing light.

Compared to all the vehicles that we had come across so far in Mexico, this bus was a vastly superior specimen. The outside of the bus was an industrial, heat-reflective silver material and the bumpers were black, custom-built, cast iron shields that looked like they were designed to blast through security gates. Attached to the roof, running full-length was a bomb-proof rack with foot-high railings to hold gear. Most impressive of all was the chassis. The whole bus was on foot-and-a-half lifts with awesome shocks and oversized knobby tires, while the undercarriage was reinforced with steel plating to protect the axles and drive train. The limo of monster trucks.

Some might have found this comforting, but I was filled with dread; I had seen the types of buses that passed as "safe" in Mexico and I had seen the grade of road that the drivers were willing to take these buses down. What was the road we were about to take to the bottom of the canyon like if this was the only vehicle deemed worthy of the trip?

There was no sign of a driver, so we found a little house down the street where a woman offered scrambled eggs, fresh tortillas, juice, and coffee from her kitchen which we ate in her sitting room off TV trays. The same cast of tourists from the ferry and the train, caught in the same backpackers orbit, joined us there.

The family who ran this make-shift diner were Tarahumara Indians, obviously more affluent than many members of the tribe who still lived in caves all around Divisadero and down in the canyon itself. The Tarahumara are related to the Apache and comprise the largest indigenous population of Northern Mexico. They call themselves *Raramuri*, "The Running People," because legend has it they can run barefoot up the shear 9,200-foot red rock walls of the Barranca del Cobre.

The sun crested the rooftops and that was the signal to saddle up and ride. As the gringos loaded onto the bus with their packs, Tarahumara started appearing from the long shadows carrying burlap sacks and boxes wrapped in brown paper bound in twine. The driver, dressed impeccably in a pressed shirt and trousers, hung off the ladder at the back of the bus and passed the locals' packages up onto the rack.

There were about fifteen passengers, half tourists. The

inside of the bus was as impressive as the exterior. It looked like an operating room. Stainless steel coping around the windows, hard cream-coloured enamel walls, and industrial non-slip rubber flooring. The seats were sturdy, covered in dark green vinyl, and were set on rubber bushings and then bolted to the floor. It was immaculate. Again I felt fear.

Exhibiting our grade-school, cool-guy savvy, Mike, Kenny, and I opted for the back seats. There was plenty of room for one double seat per passenger so we spread out. Mike managed to cram his pack into the overhead racks. Kenny and I put ours on the floor behind the last seats.

The road was potholed and rutted but clear of snow. Busosaurus rolled on effortlessly and we all settled in as best we could for the frigid dawn ride. The English tucked into their tomes and the Kiwis broke out the crib board; the Tarahumara sat inanimate, staring ahead stone-faced. After looking over several guidebooks and various maps, only one thing was clear: It was not a smart thing to hike in Barranca del Cobre.

The town we were headed toward, which may or may not have been named La Bufa, was an old silver mining town, as was the town of Batopilas—which we were supposed to find on the other side of the divide—but the mines were long closed and it seemed the only real industry in the canyon now was the growing of marijuana and opium. All the books assured us that the impoverished proprietors of these crops wouldn't blink an eye before shooting you in the face if they thought you were there to steal the crops or arrest them.

As we contemplated this information, one of the young, male Indians a few seats up broke out of his trance and started clawing at the window. The sun was up by then, but it was far from warm in the bus. He lashed at the release, trying to get the window open, palms white against the glass in an effort to slide it up. Then he stopped, bent over, his head between his knees, and spewed.

His breakfast, which appeared to be raw grains, slapped the rubber floor with authority. The odour was instantaneously noxious. The Anglos all looked up, exchanging grimaces and subtle head shakes. The people of the canyon didn't blink, didn't flinch, their eyes locked dead ahead. Kenny, in an act of desperation, tried to get his window open, putting forth an effort that was meant to seem casual and non-insulting to the man who no longer had his first meal of the day. As Mike and I giggled childishly at Kenny and the situation in general (the Jane Austen Trio was also giggling, but nervously), more frantic movement was detected near the front of the bus.

Another Tarahumara seizure—a woman this time. Another assault on an unbudging bus window. The same basic result, although this woman appeared to have had orange soda and popcorn for breakfast. And soon the rest of the tribe sprang to life. Before any of us budget travellers could properly absorb what was going on, the natives began to hurl, one by one, no longer even bothering to try their windows, just bending forward slightly at the waist, and letting it rip.

Mike and I were in stitches. The Kiwis were stunned. The English were aghast. Kenny continued to thrash at his window. Tangible tension.

Within five minutes every Indian on the bus had emptied the contents of their stomachs onto the floor and were now back into their Tarahumara trance.

Kenny finally got his window open and began to calm ever so slightly. There was a sense of stifled delirium mixed with the acrid stench of vomit. The quiet after a passing thunderstorm. It was then that the bus began to climb the gentle rise to the lip of the canyon, tilting the bus just enough to have all the semi-digested food flow freely down the non-slip rubber flooring to the back of the bus.

It was shortly after watching the flotsam tide by under my feet that I realized my backpack was on the floor.

It dawned on Kenny at the same time. We both lunged over the seat backs and yanked our packs off the ground. They were dripping—a good one-third soaked.

"This isn't right," Kenny said, quietly at first. "This isn't right." He continued to repeat it, getting louder and louder until he could easily be heard all over the bus. "This isn't right." The bus driver was glancing nervously into the rearview mirror. Even some of the Tarahumara broke their meditation to look, ice-eyed, at Kenny who was now screaming, "THIS ISN'T RIGHT!"

There was danger in the air; there was palpable craziness. I don't know if the driver picked up on it, or whether it was just a pre-planned stop, but before Kenny's head spun around on his shoulders we pulled off the road into a little one-store village. Kenny and I busted out of the back door of the bus before it came to a complete stop, dragging our sopping packs behind us.

"This isn't right," Kenny continued, but more subdued, as we inspected the damage. "This isn't right."

"Okay, Kenny, it's not right. We know, Kenny, it's wrong."

The store owner brought us a handful of paper towels that were about as absorbent as diamonds and pointed to a rusty cistern out back. We went to work mopping up our packs. Driver Pressed Pants grabbed a nasty looking broom that appeared to have been used for this very same task many times before, and herded most of the vomit out the back of the bus. He explained to Mike that Tarahumara were not used to riding in motorized vehicles and they were all extremely prone to motion sickness.

Kenny climbed the ladder at the back of the bus and I passed our packs up to him so they could dry out in the sun, which was well up and quickly warming the silver bus. We all stocked up with water and snacks before heading off again.

The bus was pungent and, even with most of the windows open, the sun beating down on us wasn't helping. Our discomfort was soon forgotten when we broached the rim of the canyon. It was like the moment on a roller coaster when you reach the top of the first pitch, right before you rush screaming down the tracks. The canyon spread out before us as far as the horizon, the bottom not yet visible behind the twists and turns of the road that skinnied its way along the cliff walls below. This road, like the Chihuahua-Pacifico railroad, was an impressive example of what man can achieve in the face of adversity, especially when there's the promise of profit at the end of it all.

From the lip, the road looked barely wide enough for goats, let alone a bus. What if another vehicle came the other way? As we drove down the first precipice the physics of the situation hit home. One side of the bus was assaulted by the branches of trees that grew from the canyon walls, the odd branch snapping through an open window making those on that side of the bus cringe. On the other side, the road could only be seen by sticking your head out the window to look down at the tires rolling inches from a very soft-looking edge.

Everyone held their breath, both in the childish way of trying to keep the bus from rolling to the bottom of the canyon in a fiery ball of crushed metal by using sheer willpower, and because the vomit smell was becoming unbearable.

From time to time the bus would come to a stop, seemingly for no reason. One of the Indians would stand, walk off the bus, grab their gear from the roof, and launch over the edge into nothingness or scramble up an invisible path into the chaparral above the road. It was impossible to imagine any place inhabitable in the area.

After about an hour, most of the Tarahumara had disembarked and the bus pulled over at a little shack perched on a flat piece of land at a hairpin turn. The scenery was undeniably brilliant, but the odour situation was detracting greatly from our enjoyment. That's when our man Kenny came through like a champion: He asked our driver if it was alright to sit up on the roof rack. Simple genius.

We, the Kiwis, and even the English, climbed the ladder with snacks and drinks and settled in up top. The sun was brilliant and the breeze kept us comfortable. All around us was a true miracle of nature. We shared food and drinks. We told stories. We snapped pictures. After the first low-hanging branch almost knocked one of the Brontës off the roof, we put a man on point to call out warnings of "Hit the deck!"

After a time, we all fell silent. Hawks circled high above, surfing the thermal currents blowing up from the canyon floor. Eventually we saw the white water that carved out this behemoth, that moved countless tonnes of rock and soil, slowly, methodically over thousands of years, still flowing, still digging ever deeper into the hard, red earth. The air became humid, tropical. Colourful birds flitted in the dense jungle foliage around us. We were nestled in our nest, each of us drinking in the moment.

This was the reason to shun the package tours, the guided expeditions. The reason we got off the beaten path.

This was the reason we travelled in the first place.

The ride to the bottom of the canyon lasted hours and we were all sad when it ended. We shook hands somewhat awkwardly, finding words hard, going our separate ways.

Pretending to Be Poor

Scott Gunning

A friend and I once spent a year pretending to be poor. We were young and travelling in Asia and wanted to be free to roam and avoid returning home for as long as we possibly could. We treated each penny as though it was our last, and so it was that we came to sleep, eat, and ride alongside those who weren't pretending.

Looking back, it seems an obscene fantasy, the self-imposed deprivation of adventure seekers eager to claim some kinship with the truly dispossessed of the world—walking up to a ticket counter and proudly demanding third-class passage, walking away from a guest house check-in because two dollars seemed absurdly expensive—playing a game that the poor would opt out of in an instant.

However, eventually you catch a glimpse of what being poor actually means and you realize that you're only strong enough to do it when it's a choice and that, were you inescapably immersed in a life of absolute poverty, you absolutely could not cope. Finally you arrive at the inevitable question, "How do they do it?" It was an Indian bus that brought me to that question.

We were to travel between the two southern Indian cities of Thiruvananthapuram (also known as Trivandrum, though I'm not certain why the place might require a second name) and Madurai—an eight-hour journey. The bus station in Trivandrum was the dusty, diesel-perfumed playground for hawkers, beggars, and wayfarers we had come to expect over the previous few months. At this particular station there were no bays or designated boarding areas for different routes. The buses pulled in randomly and it was up to travellers to identify their bus and then scramble to reach and board it before it hastily departed, trailing clouds of confusion. For some reason a lot of whistle blowing and sounding of air-horns typically accompanied this process; it was as though those empowered with these devices could not resist the urge to repeatedly shout, "Here I am, here I am" in some attempt to, at least momentarily, rise above the throng.

Although buses occasionally had English signs declaring their destinations, the majority used Malayalam and Tamil, the respective languages of the states of Kerala and Tamil Nadu. I asked the Station Master if he would identify our bus to us and he promised to point it out the moment it entered the station. We knew that we had to reach the bus as quickly as possible were we to have any hope of obtaining a seat, and our fear of being slow led us to torment the poor man by poking him in the arm and asking, "Is that it?" every time a new bus pulled into sight.

The bus he finally pointed out was already full as it entered the station. This was not unusual and typically the numbers exiting balanced somewhat with the numbers boarding, allowing all riders to travel in conditions that were at least tolerably intolerable. On this ride, things were to be different. A few travellers trickled off the bus and were nearly driven back on board by the crush of people attempting to get into the packed vehicle. Those who disembarked cannot be said to have really created more room on board, only to have negligibly shifted the degree of overcrowding.

Seemingly everyone waiting to board decided they were destined to fill one of the handful of vacated spots, spots that could only have existed through some strange compression of flesh, or acrobatic gut sucking, or anomalies of physics whereby Newton's laws were temporarily suspended, or perhaps through the intervention of Vishnu the Preserver, allowing wayward knees, arms, and shoulders to slip through temporal rifts and exist in a dimension dedicated to the deliverance of those desperate to get somewhere on this horrendously hot day.

The improbability of the scene before me was staggering. I thought of a dozen circus clowns piling into a tiny fire engine, and then I thought of these clowns attempting an eight-hour journey in their fire engine, and then I thought of this journey taking place in thirty-eight-degree heat and then I thought that, on the whole, I would rather be on that fire engine, with those clowns, in that heat, than on this bus. And then we rushed the door hoping that Vishnu would find a little more room in his hopefully-not-so-far-off dimension of preservation.

It would be impossible to describe any single bus I encountered as a typical Indian bus. They defied categorization entirely—windows, no windows, broken windows; bench seats, reclining seats, no seats, broken seats; luggage stored on the roof, at your feet, on overhead racks, or next to the driver; animal-accommodating buses, animal-excluding buses; video coaches showing three-hour Bollywood extravaganzas one after another; or coaches wired for sound blaring the latest and greatest in Hindi pop at volumes rendering everything dissonant and distorted in seemingly perfect sympathy with the surrounding chaos.

This particular example was blessedly free of any and all multimedia features (torments for which passengers inexplicably paid more) and was simply a beat-up, windowless, state-run transport. There was, however, one feature that was unlike any I had seen before. The front of the bus was sectioned off by a sort of wire cage, and the relatively large area to the left of the driver was free of seats and seemed to be intended for luggage storage. (In India, the driver is situated on the right-hand side of the vehicle as, theoretically at least, traffic travels on the left; few drivers, however, actually permit this convention to stifle their creativity and driving typically takes place on the part of the road that looks most appealing at any given moment with right-of-way instantaneously calculated using the variables of vehicle size and air-horn volume.)

One can imagine a variety of rationales for such a configuration: luggage theft is common in India and the caged-off section would not be accessible to thieves; the driver would also be protected from jostling by the mob he carried or assaults by those upset by his driving (I had heard a number of stories about drivers assaulted in recompense for terror provoked); etc. Evidently, however, those sufficiently privileged to get jobs designing buses in India have no call to actually use public transport, or the purpose that this caged area would ultimately serve would have been foreseen—it was standing room.

This area was packed with riders, many pressed up against the front window while others rode virtually in the lap of the driver. For my part, I found a small space between the back of the driver's seat and the cage that I was able to wedge myself into. Because of the way the driver's seat was angled, there was no room to stand and I had to shuffle in behind the seat in a crouch. I twisted my torso so that my shoulders were square with the back of the seat while my knees were together and on my left. My arms were stretched out to the side and slightly behind me so I could knit my fingers into the cage for additional support as we bumped along the road, and I let my head fall forward so that it was resting on the back of the driver's seat. I suppose if you crucified someone in a very narrow room with an exceedingly low ceiling, this is the posture they would be forced into.

In the bedlam of boarding, I had been separated from my friend and, corkscrewing my neck to look over my shoulder, I tried to confirm that he had made it into the passenger section to my rear. It was nearly impossible to see anything from my vantage point, but as the bus bounced and swayed along the potholed road the passengers bounced and swayed with it and, from time to time, all this movement conspired to afford me a glimpse of my friend. He didn't look good. He was standing in the crush of the aisle and, without a readily available handhold, seemed to be maintaining his balance only through the support of the bodies pressing against him. He was pale, his face beaded with sweat. Apparently, I was lucky.

I had a space that was exclusively mine, something to hold

onto, a place to rest my head, and—perhaps most importantly—I enjoyed the good fortune of being unable to see the road ahead. This last perk made it somewhat easier to try to relax and forge some fragile peace with my physical discomfort. I thought of the unfortunates whose faces were pasted to the front window, living through the horrors of a thousand narrowly averted head-on collisions.

Many Indian roads are so narrow that they scarcely accommodate the combined widths of two buses, and the drivers seem to have developed a curious strategy for creating more room. They steer into each other's lanes slightly and then, at the last possible moment, steer back into their own so that the pass takes place at a slight angle. I must confess, I never quite understood how this tactic made passing easier. Perhaps it just made it more likely that if a collision did occur it would not be of the head-on variety, thus giving the drivers a better chance of survival with a less catastrophic glancing blow. Maybe the drivers felt that they had to claim as much pavement as possible prior to the pass to avoid being blown off the road. Whatever the explanation, those with their faces pressed to the front window must have felt profound fear every time the drivers steered toward one another like a couple of suicidal maniacs playing a bizarre game of chicken with other people's lives. Possibly, it *was* simply a bizarre game of chicken.

As the trip wore on, however, these small consolations slowly lost their consoling power and I began to feel overwhelmed by my claustrophobic immobility. The pain in my knees made me forget those with their faces pasted to the front window, and the knots in my back made me forget those with nothing to hold onto, and the nausea inspired by the closeness and the heat made me forget that I was lucky.

I was ready to get off this touring terror at the next possible opportunity. It was hard to believe that conditions this difficult were not a component of some disaster or bizarre and rare misfortune, but were simply a mundane feature of everyday life encountered or avoided through an accident of birth. If you were poor and had to go somewhere—across town or across the country—these were the conditions you could expect to encounter, perhaps daily, over the course of a lifetime. There wasn't, of course, any screaming or crying on board and the expressions on the faces of those around me were largely impassive. They had to be experiencing pain or discomfort similar to mine, but they seemed to be facing the situation with an equanimity I could not find. The question was before me now: How did they do it?

I was travelling in the home of yoga. The image of a yogi effortlessly folding himself into a tiny glass box floated into my mind and I thought what a boon this skill—a Darwinian adaptation for a mass transit culture—would be on an Indian bus journey.

I looked back through the cage and again spotted my friend. His condition seemed to have deteriorated. He was now completely drained of colour, his eyes sunken as though in retreat from the scene before them. I was confident that, could I get his attention, he would agree that we should get off the bus. Suddenly, though, he fainted and in doing so, provided me with the answer to my question. A seat was immediately vacated and he was lifted up and placed in it by our obviously concerned and caring fellow passengers. I stopped worrying about my knees and my back and, once again, I felt lucky.

With a place to sit my friend recovered quickly, but when he tried to surrender his seat those around him would have none of it—enough drama for one journey, I suppose. The only attention I received came from a handful of people I caught enviously eyeing the luxurious hideaway I occupied. I silently vowed to offer it up without hesitation should any of those around me require assistance. A few hours later we got off the bus in Madurai. It felt good to stretch my legs.

Jungle Train: Travels in Malaysia

Ariel Gordon

It is morning, too early to contemplate anything but the shape of clasped pillows and the precise angle of the sun through the windows, but we are awake. We sit at the station with our squat bags and our sodden expectations and, to our great relief, the golden buds of the nearby mosque seem more like flowers about to unfold than insistent fists of stone.

We are leaving Taman Negara National Park via the town of Kuala Lipis, a word that deserves to be mouthed reverently, to be tasted, but this is the only chance we will have to say it, as our only experience of this place will be its train station.

We are leaving behind the river we putt-putted along in wooden boats motored by sullen guides from the village. We are leaving behind the mist that was caught in the tops of the trees most days, filtering down through the atmosphere and infiltrating our clothes by mid-morning.

There is much reminiscing about the cicadas that crash-landed on light fixtures in our dorm-style lodgings, figuring they were potential mates. We cite nameless insects, as big as the face of my watch, that would land on the mosquito netting around my bed. One got into the path of the fan and was shredded, spraying the English girl in the next bunk with bug blood. She shrieked and carried on, forcing us to listen to her complain. I let the cloud of mosquito netting descend, enjoying my enclosed space, the firmness of the bunk, the jungle visible through the open slats.

The train will come, we are told. Ten hours from here to there.

There, at this moment, means Kota Bharu, a Muslim enclave to the northeast. It will mean watching Muslim gentlemen in the restaurant near the train station, in their crocheted white fezes, thin white dress shirts, and sarongs in the palest of shades. It will mean being mesmerized by their fingers, nearly obscured by the rings they wear, big things with crude settings and semi-precious stones, as they transmit their food to their mouths. We will try to imitate them—two fingers to hold the naan, one to rip patches from it, then the rest to deftly scoop curry—but will only smear ourselves with food.

But this is later.

Right now, all we have are the train tracks and the mosque across from the train station. The roof has spiky dragons dancing along its spine that will never quite meet, laughing open flowers, and upswept palms. And always, with these faded human constructions, there are geckos flattened like bad tattoos against the walls.

The jungle train comes and the foreigners, with their thin English-language newspapers and bottles of water, all settle in the same car. This is first class, where the floor is reassuringly solid, not like the car down the line that allows views of the tracks between your feet. We begin to move, leaving behind the station for the country—brown hills ridged like stairs appear and rusty metal bridges reaching over milk-coloured rivers peek between stands of palms and other resplendent greenery.

An older gentleman with skin the colour of coffee, a pink plastic sack thrown over one shoulder, gets on the train and sits opposite me. We pass a smile between us and I see that his teeth are long like ivory in his mouth, that some are missing. I offer him jackfruit but he declines, waving one hand, so I politely scan the trees out the window. When he gets up a few stops later, we smile again, the social niceties observed. I am a little disappointed—but that shifts to surprise when he stops in front of me, planting his feet firmly on the floor, and digs in his bag, his arm disappearing up to the elbow. When he pulls his arm out, his palm is full of green mango. He hands it to me and then his eyes are busy on my cheeks, which are burning with pleasure. I hold the fruit to my nose, amazed by the warmth and fragrance of it, and crack a huge smile. He nods, then hops off the train in the midst of a pair of wet water buffalo who have been racing the train along the length of their paddy. He makes for the mountains, unconcerned, undoubtedly crossing beneath other horns, other wet hides.

At the next stop, schoolboys in white dress shirts and Adidas shorts or long pants climb on. For them, this is a commuter train, a vehicle to get them from duty to obligation and back. The boys scan the crowd lazily and discuss us in Malay. They form a ragtag huddle, smiles on their narrow faces, and then in the manner of customs agents, spend the rest of their trip collecting signatures from all the tourists, somebody's Hello Kitty notebook passed from hand to hand.

When we reach the next dot on the map, the boys file off the train, giggling and punching each other's bony shoulders. They are replaced by vendors selling hardboiled quail eggs, speckled brown and white, and chunks of fruit in the ubiquitous Asian baggie. We try the fruit, spending long moments trying to place the shapes, the flavours. A man with ginger-coloured hair and bubbles of sunburnt skin on his nose spies what we are eating and laughs. He starts telling us stories about jackfruit, how it is covered in spikes, how it grows so big armies have used it as catapult ammunition. The his eyes roll to the ceiling as he tries to find just the right word to describe the smell of its equally spiky cousin, durian.

"Cat piss," he says eventually.

Midway through our trip, the train comes to a complete stop, lingering at a station for a good half hour. There is the usual emptying and filling of the seats in the cars around us, the manhandling of packages tied with string, the averting of eyes by girls in chadors, a school logo picked out carefully in embroidery on their uniforms.

The conductor has been about, smiling at us all like a bachelor uncle, and we are just about to be on our way again when the woman dressed in orange the colour of marigolds reboards the train. Her daughter follows her, naked, leaving wet footprints on the floor of the train. The marigold woman hoists her up so that she can stand and be towelled off on the seat. The girl, her wrists and ankles ringed with gold chains, stares at me as if to say, Ah . . . how lovely to have a bath in the middle of our trip, even if it was in the sink of the women's washroom.

No one else seems to find this spectacle remarkable and I laugh out loud at the absurdity of it, producing bursts of staccato laughter that float away into the sky.

Toward evening, I grab the pack of Indonesian clove cigarettes and make for the alcove between cars, propping open one of the doors so I can watch the jungle as it passes, getting windblown as I peer into the faces of the mountains. The villages, made of corrugated metal and bamboo, or concrete and brick, cluster around the stations. A Malay university professor joins me there, smiling slyly as he offers compliments like clusters of linguistic flowers.

I return to my seat and find the pleasant fatigue of travel, the lull that allows you to find the rhythm of the thing, to move with it and glide.

Later, I will think about how the sway of the train is like the movement of an animal, its haunches moving underneath us. I will notice how the schoolgirls lift their long skirts over the grasses on the paths that lead them home, how the landscape forces them to show a little leg.

But first, I will look up and return to the mist and the faint blue skies of this morning. I will allow myself to sleep, supported on all sides by other travellers. I will try to dream of something more fantastic than this.

Good Luc': A Cautionary Thai Tale

Ian Cockfield

After an hour in the taxi, I knew I'd made a mistake. Siriporn was in the front talking Thai to the driver while I sat in the back, my Lonely Planet guidebook open, trying to learn a bit more of the language. Siriporn's voice rose—he seemed angry about something.

"Everything okay?" I asked.

Siriporn turned to face me. "Ve'y big problem. The driver, he los'."

We were stuck in traffic on one of the expressways winding through Bangkok. It was December, the cool season according to the book, but a hot, sticky breeze was blowing in through the taxi's open windows. I was covered in a sheen of grimy sweat—the bandanna I was using to wipe down my forehead and chest was coming away black.

I consulted my book. "*Khun poot len*"—You are joking?

Now the driver turned around. He was an avuncular sort, with a kind, round face and large Buddha ears. In halting English he explained how he'd been driving taxi since he was a young man like me, but after thirty years of breathing in leaded car exhaust, his memory was not like it used to be. "Too many car, it no good," he concluded.

"Do you need a map?"

"Wha' map?" asked Siriporn.

I unfolded my Bangkok bus map ("If you don't speak Thai just point to the Thai word of your destination")—which, along with a cheap sarong, prickly heat powder, and Rizla rolling papers is one of the few necessities for backpacking around Thailand—and passed it up front. Siriporn began flipping the map this way and that, seemingly reading out street names at random while the driver kept shaking his head. I asked him what the matter was. "All these road, same same but differen'." I guess they figured out where we were, however, because we soon turned off the expressway and began heading in a new direction.

I had spent that morning wandering through the area bordering Wat Phra Keo, the royal temple complex next to the Grand Palace. I came upon a road where, on either side, hawkers seated on mats sold small devotional statues, ecclesiastic supplies and pendants with stylized Thai script surrounding emaciated monks in lotus position. The sidewalks were overflowing with local collectors going from one stand to the next, peering with their magnifying glasses at the tiny figures nestled in plastic boxes. One of the pendants immediately caught my attention—there was something calming about the emotionless gaze of the deep-set eyes, a face beyond this world of suffering and attachment—the expression of awakened mind. Besides, it was a cheap souvenir. So for a few baht I soon had an effigy of a real Thai monk named Pla Pawanah Kosun Terah hanging by a piece of string from around my neck.

I was thirsty and ducked into a café for an ice coffee. The entire front of the place opened on to the street. It was empty inside, a few plastic tables and chairs strewn about. On the grimy walls, framed photographs of the king and royal family alternated with washed-out posters of the Swiss Alps. Soon after I ordered, a Thai man in a pressed silk shirt and black pants sat down at my table. He opened up his handbag, took out a pack of Salem menthols and a Zippo lighter, and introduced himself as Siriporn.

I had been travelling in Asia for a few months at this point and had developed a wariness when approached by locals. Too many instances of students showing off rudimentary English skills ("What is your good name?" "What is your good country?") while their friends giggled nearby, and touts imploring me to visit their "uncle's" (or "brother's" or "cousin's") carpet factory/jewellery shop/guesthouse, had left me jaded.

This man, however, with his sleek foreign watch, chunky gold rings, and confident smile, was different. He asked me where I was from, and when I replied Canada, he seemed surprised—his sister, a nurse, had just got her Canadian work permit and was leaving for Calgary in a few days. Would I mind meeting her? She had so many questions. "You go wit' me now. We come bac' soon."

After indulging my own peripatetic pursuits for so long, the thought of being *useful* and helping this woman learn about *my country* was very tempting. I said yes.

Siriporn paid for my coffee—being on a tight budget I didn't argue—and we headed for the street. He flagged down a taxi and we got in. When the driver didn't turn on the meter, I pointed it out to Siriporn. "Is okay my frien', I pay, I pay."

Siriporn handed back my map. I think he sensed my growing apprehension about how long the trip was taking, because he suddenly launched into a convoluted monologue having something to do with "good love," "strong man," and a cream called "Champ" that soon had the taxi driver laughing so hard he began coughing up phlegm.

When the taxi driver sensed I wasn't quite getting it, he turned around and thrust a clenched fist into the air. "Champ," he explained, "make you coc' hard long time." I didn't bother looking in the Lonely Planet for a suitable response.

Bangkok, the City of Angels or *Krung Thep* to the locals, is a sprawling city of seven million people spread over three hundred square kilometres of swampland (making subways impossible). It has some of the worst traffic in Asia—the twenty-five kilometre ride in from the Don Muang airport often exceeds two hours—and that's by shuttle bus. At most major intersections, white-gloved military-esque traffic cops with oversized reflective sunglasses and surgical masks direct the crush of vehicles. The public ferries and boat traffic along the muddy Chao Phraya river and the many *klongs* is almost as chaotic.

One of the best ways to travel short distances is the *tuk-tuk*, a motorized *samlor* (three-wheeler) named after the noise its two-stroke engine makes. The driver sits astride the engine up front, steering with a motorcycle-like handlebar. There's room for two passengers on the back seat. The sides are open, a fabric top offering a modicum of protection from the monsoon rains. They are often decorated with an assortment of lights, horns, stickers, customized fabrics, and other embellishments. They're noisy, breezy, often driven at terrifying speeds, but allow the passenger an unparalleled feeling of being *right there*. They're also easy to find.

The night before, I found myself on one of these tuk-tuks with a Danish woman named Marianne racing Ben-Hur-like down Rama IV Road, her two friends right behind in another tuk-tuk urging their driver to go "more faster, more faster" while waving a fistful of Thai baht in the air. They had just arrived from less permissive Indonesia and wanted to check out one of the infamous Patpong sex shows, and felt that having a guy along would make things more comfortable. I agreed, thinking that having them along would make *me* more comfortable. And so, around 11 p.m., after each popping an over-the-counter Thai amphetamine and puffing back a few bong hits at the guesthouse, off we went. Soon we were flying through intersections, the signs and neon lights of the passing stores and temples a resplendent Plasticine blur.

The red-light district of Patpong consists of two short streets overflowing with go-go bars, massage parlours, clubs featuring "fucky-fucky" shows, and stalls selling all manner of pirated and counterfeit goods. Over a few exorbitantly priced Singha beers at a place with stained concrete walls and a few dismal, coloured lights, we looked on as a procession of bored, naked Thai women used their vaginas to perform feats ranging from the banal (smoking half a pack of cigarettes), through the spectacular (arcing bananas a good ten metres across the room), to the truly astounding: After pulling out a string of pins from her genitals, one young woman lay down on the floor, emptied a full litre bottle of Coca-Cola into her womb, then stood up, squatted, and proceeded to fill one empty bottle with *water*, then *another* with the original Coke, like some strange assembly-line flesh machine.

The Thais are about the friendliest people I've ever met (this despite being ardent carnivores, the founders of a particularly vicious school of kick-boxing, and sharing borders with several of the most brutal dictatorships of this century).

Two weeks before, I'd been in the northwest riding in a *songthaew* on my way to trek among the hill tribes near Mae Hong Son. A songthaew literally means "two rows," and most often consists of an Isuzu pickup with a covered back and a row of benches down each side with enough room in between to hold bags of produce, large blocks of ice wrapped in burlap, or a bound pig or two. It's one of the best ways to meet locals, squished as you invariably are in the back (only the lucky get to ride up front with the driver), your knees almost touching the person opposite. There's not much to look at either, except one another. Halfway through the trip, I felt something rubbing my leg just below my shorts. I looked over and met the beaming smile of an old, wizened Thai man, his mouth stained blood-red from chewing betel nut. He continued looking at me as he ran his hand up and down the thick hair of my Canadian thigh. Then he took my hand, placed it on his smooth, tropical skin, and moved it back and forth as if to say, Look how different we are!

Of course, there were dangers for the traveller as well. A Brit told me he'd been on a tourist bus headed for one of the southern beaches in the Gulf of Thailand, enjoying the "in-flight" videos, free meal, and many complimentary drinks, only to wake up several hours later with a severe headache. The bus was parked in the middle of a coconut plantation—the driver and attendant nowhere to be seen. He had no idea how they'd got there. As the other tourists slowly regained consciousness, it was discovered that everyone's money belts and knapsacks had been razored open and emptied. He was the only lucky one to still have his passport and travellers' cheques because he'd been stupid enough to leave his valuables in his backpack strapped to the roof rack.

Then there were the more sobering accounts of people vanishing in the jungle, late-night knife-point abductions from beach huts, and the oft-repeated "myth" of young men waking up in bathtubs full of ice *sans* kidney.

Almost two hours after we left the café, the taxi finally stopped. We seemed to be in a residential neighbourhood. Sooty stucco and poured concrete buildings had given way to wood houses behind high brick fences with glass shards embedded along the tops. Across the street in a dusty field strewn with discarded water bottles, a small group of motorcycle taxi drivers in numbered vests and flip-flops were kicking a rattan ball back and forth over a net playing *sepak ta kraw*—a traditional game resembling a mix of hacky-sack and volleyball. There were no other people around.

Siriporn handed the driver some baht and got out of the taxi. I grabbed my knapsack, said "Khop khoon khrap" to the smiling driver and followed Siriporn through the iron gate of a nearby house. Siriporn locked the gate behind us and led me around back to a wooden porch overhanging a large pond choked with water lilies and hyacinth, and surrounded by an impenetrable tangle of palms and banana trees.

Siriporn indicated a bench by a Formica table under the shade of the corrugated tin roof. "You wan' Spri'? You wan' Coke?"

"Sprite," I answered. He threw open the doors separating the porch from the house and walked in. Siriporn was obviously doing alright for himself: The place consisted of an open main room with several doors off to the side, a few pieces of ornately carved teak furniture about, the kitchen in one corner, an altar with a graceful bronze Buddha in another. But no sister. After the long trip out, I'd almost forgotten about her.

When Siriporn reappeared with the two Sprites, I asked him where she was. "She mus' be ou'. Is okay, you stay, you wai' for my sister."

To pass the time we chatted about my travels in Thailand—where I'd gone, what I did, what I thought. Siriporn kept looking up at the clock every so often, but there was no more mention of his sister, or what kind of information she wanted to know. The afternoon slowly slipped away.

At one point I got up to go to the toilet. Siriporn pointed to one of the doors off the main room. When I was washing my hands in the bathroom, casually looking about, it struck me that there was nothing at all to indicate a woman lived there. Hadn't Siriporn told me she'd been staying with him for the past few months while she applied for the work permit?

On my way back to the porch, I scanned the main room. Again, no sign: no pictures of a Thai woman in uniform, no family portraits, no happy brother and sister shots—nothing. That was when the other man showed up.

The man was a younger, wiry version of Siriporn, his red silk shirt partially unbuttoned, blue swirls of tattoos on his chest. They reminded me of the engraved writing and symbols on the pendant I had bought earlier that day (was it really just a few hours ago?). His eyes were obscured by a pair of dark sunglasses. It was soon apparent that he was not the smiling kind.

Siriporn didn't introduce me to the man, but quickly led him into the main room where they sat side by side on a teak settee with elaborately embroidered pillows. I stayed seated on the hard bench out on the porch and started chain-smoking Krong Thip cigarettes, absently leafing through my Lonely Planet guide, trying to figure out what I should do. I looked over at the pair—they seemed to be discussing something serious, every so often casting a glance my way.

I realized I didn't know a thing about these people. I hadn't even bothered to ask Siriporn what he did for a living. I was only there out of selfishness—that damn karmic attachment again! I grabbed the little monk hanging around my neck, but all I could seem to concentrate on was the sweat pooling under my money belt.

Then I started to get really scared. Here I was, a *farang*—an outsider. No one knew I was there. *I* didn't even know where I was. And who would even care?

I had to get out of there.

"Siriporn, I must leave now," I said, trying to sound calm.

Siriporn turned to me, squinting into the sunlight from outside. "Is okay, you can stay tonigh'. You wan' another Spri'?"

I made up an excuse about meeting some friends, some really *good* friends, at the General Post Office. "They'll be very worried if I'm late," I assured Siriporn.

"You wai' for my sister."

"I really can't. *Mai pen rai*—So it goes," I said, and shoved my guidebook into my knapsack, stood up, and started heading for the path by the side of the house. Just before disappearing around the corner I thanked him for the drink.

"Ian?"

I stopped. It was the first time he'd used my name since I'd introduced myself at the café.

Siriporn gave me a quick wave of his hand. "Good luc'."

The other man walked me around front, unlocked the gate, and pointed to the motorcycle taxi stand after handing me some baht.

An hour later I was finally on a city bus back to Khao San Road and my guesthouse. I looked out the window at the traffic rumbling all around, the people busy rushing by on the crowded sidewalks, everyone immersed in their own bubbles of life. As the ticket collector came down the aisle toward me, clacking her metal change box, I took a deep breath. I held it. Oh, how sweet that smell of exhaust.

Riding Shotgun

John Vigna

The trip to Bhuj was twenty-two hours on a dusty regular STC bus. Bhuj is the major town in Kutch—the westernmost part of the state of Gujarat—a peninsula landlocked between the Sind and Thar deserts near the Pakistan border, a desolate region of black mudflats and tawny salt crust. Bhuj attracted me because of its remoteness from the tourist trail of haggard hippies and enlightened travellers—the trippies that I had encountered throughout India.

There was little information on Bhuj, which created more desire for me to see it. I gleaned sparse bits of information from guidebooks, the odd lone traveller, and locals. I entertained fantasies about Bhuj, an ancient walled town where in the past the gates were locked each night from dusk to dawn. The maze-like streets were rumoured to be fascinating for exploring—walls within walls, intricate gateways, old palaces, and brightly decorated temples. I imagined *The Arabian*

Nights: camel herds floating on the shimmering haze of baked earth, strings of donkeys jingling by, sheep and goats fussing at the meagre scrub under the eyes of turbaned boys, and mongooses scuttling over dusty paths. Thatched mud houses painted with brilliant patterns. The women as bright as parakeets sitting outside their homes, weaving and embroidering blouses, skirts, and shawls.

The bus seats were hard wooden benches. I chose a regular bus, instead of the deluxe air con buses with high-backed padded seats that most travellers used, despite the fact that I get car-sick easily. I reasoned it would bring me closer to the locals since it was the cheapest form of transport available. Most importantly though, they did not play videos or blare indecipherable Bollywood music through distorted speakers. Those were the sorts of things that could make a person sick.

I sat next to a grimy window and laid my backpack on the seat next to me to create space for myself. I didn't want to tie it to the top of the bus where I couldn't see it for the duration of the trip. There were mounds of baggage crammed in the aisles; more luggage was strapped on top of the bus with frayed ropes. Several men wrapped in dirty shawls sat with the luggage on the roof—the "upper class" deck. I was glad to have my pack next to me.

The heat beat down as we descended from the cool slopes of Mt. Abu, a popular resort among young Indian honeymooners, onto the mud and salt flats of Kutch. I sat behind the driver with an empty plastic bag between my legs, just in case. My legs were crammed up against the mangled chain link fence that separated me from the driver. His assistant had wild eyes and a pink scarf tied around his head. He snorted some kind of substance from a dark plastic bag, lit bidis and passed them to the driver. Whenever the driver slowed, which was rare, the brakes squealed like fighting cats. Sitting behind the driver seemed like the safest place.

We stopped at the base of Mt. Abu and picked up a load of wizened villagers. A soldier drunk on *arak*, a distilled rice liquor, clear and deadly, climbed on board. He stumbled toward me, holding the side of the bench for support.

He motioned toward my backpack, waving his gleaming Kalashnikov back and forth. I jammed the pack between my legs on the floor. He leaned the rifle against my shoulder. "It is loaded," he reassured me before falling asleep, his head resting on my shoulder. I gently pushed him away. He opened a bloodshot eye and turned away, a trail of arak fumes assaulting my nostrils. The cool barrel of his gun rested against my cheek. Whenever the bus stopped for chai breaks, I'd blurt out "Shotgun" to no one in particular, and walk quickly back to my seat. I quickly grew bored of this by the second stop, two hours into the ride. I entertained visions of Russian roulette, wondering if the locals had a different version. But this is the land of Gandhi. There's no such game here. Catching any sleep next to a drunk and snoring soldier with a loaded AK-47 was impossible.

The driver kept hammering the horn repeatedly. Near-death experiences rushed toward us—he seemed to be playing chicken with the swarming mass of oncoming vehicles, animals, and people. I'd read that the average Indian driver used their horn twenty to thirty times per kilometre, which added up considerably over a twenty-two-hour journey.

A greasy bath of fine sand and diesel fumes filtered through the open windows. If I had to get sick, I knew I couldn't puke out the windows—I'd end up spraying the people sitting behind me. But every time I stuck my head out to gulp some fresh air, the sight of the wide streams of vomit and red betel nut juice staining the sides of the bus nearly made me hurl. I looked down at my bag. I felt grit between my teeth and my stomach was tight with tension. The other passengers were smoking or sleeping.

I grew exhausted using "body English" to help the driver stay on the road—which turned out to be useless—because he soon blared his horn, swerved to avoid a cow, and ploughed into a bony old man riding a bicycle. The brakes howled. Dust filled the bus. All of us were silent for a moment. And then the coughing began. The driver leapt out the window and sprinted into the desert, a tiny dot fading into the horizon, and then he disappeared.

It is estimated that there are roughly 150 road deaths every day in India, which works out to be around 55,000 per year. Many of these accidents are of the hit-and-run variety. Drivers routinely bolt after hitting someone since lynch mobs can assemble quickly, even if the driver is not at fault. No one ran after our driver when he absconded.

The pink-scarved assistant began shouting in Hindi and rushed out the door. I climbed over the sleeping soldier, pushing his gun toward him. He didn't move. The rest of the bus emptied out quickly and we stood looking at the man. A red pool of arterial blood spread across the dust. Two men began fiddling with the mangled bike, trying to straighten out the handlebars. The seat post was twisted and bent over like a wilted plant. It was impossible to avoid staring at the man on the ground—he looked as if he was sleeping with his eyes open—so peaceful and quiet. His face, a road map of lifelines, seemed to melt and soften into the dirt. My feet were nailed to the ground. A child squatted to pee nearby. I kept staring at the man, thinking he would snap out of it, get up, brush himself off, and get back on his bike.

The assistant declared that he was the man's "uncle," which seemed to give him the right to begin searching through the man's pockets. No one moved. We stood and stared stupidly at the man whose blood mixed with the dust and was absorbed by the earth. There was some chatter and pointing toward where our driver had run.

I had no idea what death looked like. I'd never seen it before. Panic rose in my throat. I needed to do something. I ran to the bus and got a first aid kit out of my backpack. When I returned, the crowd had dispersed and the assistant ordered us to push the bus out of the ditch. The man lay uncovered.

"We can't just go, we have to help him," I said.

"Yes," replied the assistant, his eyes huge, jittery.

"We have to help him," I tried again, raising my arms.

"He's dead. There is nothing to do."

"We should wait for the police."

"No police. There is nothing to do. Life is very cheap, like everything else in India."

"Shouldn't we at least cover him up?" I asked.

"Why?"

I looked around at the ancient desert—carts pulled by oxen, carts pulled by humans, sari-clad labourers, men squatting and smoking disinterestedly. A swaying crowd of camels burping and farting as they stumbled past, dust motes sparkling in the harsh light. The likelihood of a hospital, or any town for that matter, being nearby seemed remote. I wondered where our driver was. No one seemed concerned. I joined the men push-starting the bus. Everyone smiled and laughed as dense black diesel fumes belched out the rear. I ducked when it backfired. More laughter. How I envied the soldier, still sleeping with a loaded gun against his head on the bus.

The assistant took over the driving, his mysterious baggie moving back and forth to his nose throughout the night, the glowing embers of his bidi visible in the dark. I closed my eyes. The bus veered off, horn blaring. My eyes shot open. My watch read 4:12 a.m. We stopped to eat at a brightly lit open-air restaurant. Truck drivers dozed on charpoys, bus passengers ordered food and ate quickly. I watched the assistant eat, laugh, and joke with the owners of the restaurant. He slapped them on the back and walked toward the bus. The other passengers followed suit. The roads were still crammed with hordes of vehicles, pedestrians, unlit carts and trucks, or worse, trucks with their high beams on. I couldn't see our headlights in the darkness; we seemed to be driving without them. Throughout the night I counted horn blasts, wondering what had become of the dead man, how old he was, where the driver had run to.

At dawn, an energetic merchant boarded the bus. He stood in the aisle, holding up clear bottles with green liquid inside. He was way too animated for six a.m., speaking rapidly in Hindi, rubbing his belly, pointing to his head, thumping his chest. Most of the passengers were laughing. Everyone was awake, including the soldier, who was the first to buy a bottle. Without warning, everyone began handing over fistfuls of rupees to the salesman. Some people bought two bottles. I asked the soldier what the fuss was about. He replied that this was the bottle of life. It had magical properties to live a long and healthy life.

"You don't really believe that, do you?" I replied.

"Yes, of course. Why not? What is wrong with you?"

His gun fell against my shoulder when he held up the unsealed bottle in the soft morning light. The contents were green and murky, with brown particles floating around. He opened the cap and handed it to me. I shook my head.

"As you wish," he said, and then drank half the bottle. The smell made me gag. He screwed the cap back on. I looked around and saw that everyone was taking sips of the stuff. I broke into a sweat and leaned my face out the window. Nausea gripped me. I opened the plastic bag between my legs and took deep breaths, murmuring to myself not to get sick.

The bus stopped to let off the salesman. He handed a bottle to the assistant and bid him farewell: "Namaste," *I salute the Divine that lives in you.* The assistant took a long drink, put the bus into gear, and blared his horn as he weaved in and out of the crowded road.

Late the next afternoon, the bus arrived—inexplicably—in Bhujat, the airfield north of town. Everyone chatted excitedly. The airfield was on a military base that protected the border with Pakistan. The soldier was the first off the bus, his gun over his shoulder. The assistant was next. The rest of us followed. I was pleased that I didn't get sick. Next time, I promised myself, I would take the train. I was done with STC buses. Or maybe I'd take a sleeper bus. Those sounded interesting, complete with bunk beds. On the way out of the bus stand I passed a notice that read, "The more you sweat in peace, the less you bleed in war." I read it twice to make sure. *The more you sweat in peace, the less you bleed in war*. I was in Gandhi's state now, a place of passive resistance.

NON-TRANSFERABLE

The Adventures of Red Hornet

Nicole Bohn

The Hood

I am back on MUNI, San Francisco's municipal bus system, for the first time in almost three weeks. I am free again, back from Christmas in Wisconsin, and I have my wheels once more. As of today I have a new and improved electric wheelchair—a three-wheeled scooter that I call the Red Hornet. I call it that because when we are in symbiotic relationship, I have superpowers. I can get places I wouldn't be able to go otherwise, the candy-apple shine draws people to me I wouldn't ordinarily talk to, and I meet people upside down—I notice feet first, then faces. This helps me see clearly.

I live in an area of San Francisco that city supervisors and other politically correct types call the Western Addition. Like they're fooling anyone. It's "The Hood." Tonight, the MUNI driver is detained at Fillmore and Eddy while two brothers finish their conversation in the middle of the street. A jolly-looking Latino boards and sits in the front. Chloe and her mom board after him. I like Chloe. She is five and has pretty, black, mischievous eyes and long black hair and always says hi when she sees me. Her mom has frizzy blonde hair with black roots and is a chain smoker and never says hi. I don't take this personally. I'm sure she's thinking about cigarettes.

The driver honks. The taller brother gives the driver the finger and we are detained still. The Latino guy notices me and smiles. "Hey, amiga! How you been?"

"Good," I say. Chloe waves at me and I wave back.

"You remember me, amiga? I been in San Diego for three weeks. How you been?"

I do not remember him but smile the way my dad smiles when he has no idea what was just said.

"You got a boyfriend yet?"

Now I remember him. Between MUNI patrons and cabbies and an ex-"not boyfriend," I was proposed to at least four times in 2002, and questioned about my marital status at least a dozen times again. Every time this happens it surprises me. I am a not thin, not heavy, almost-thirty-year-old with cerebral palsy. In 2003, I will keep better track of this phenomenon. Perhaps I can add "Collects Marriage Proposals" to my list of superpowers.

Tonight, I am in a good mood and play along. The Latino is friendly and in general I am attracted to Latin men, although this one is a little too Cheech Marin for me. "Nope," I say.

"You still not married?"

I hold up my hands and wiggle my fingers, which are indeed unadorned. He hangs his head and shakes it. The bus is making progress now. We pass the Goldlane grocery store; at least I think it's a grocery store. Huge posters on the windows boast bananas at sixty-nine cents a pound but I can't really see in, and no one ever seems to come out. I like to think that the Goldlane is really a CIA safehouse. Behind that questionable-looking, run-down exterior there just might be another kind of adventure waiting to unfold in my neighbourhood.

The Latino guy is talking to Chloe's mom. "Remember me?" he says. "I bummed a cigarette off you three weeks ago!"

"Oh, yeah, yeah." she says. This may be the first time I have ever seen Chloe's mom smile. Chloe is holding a drawing of two stick figures on swings. "Chloe" it says under one swing; "Tommy" it says under the other. I look for a heart drawn between the two, but do not see one.

The next stop is mine. Amigo swings his feet onto the seat so that Red Hornet and I can pass. I thank him for this. "You sure are a pretty girl," he says.

I turn onto the wheelchair lift and give Red Hornet a little too much juice. I hit the safety gate on the lift quite suddenly. I am thankful for the safety gate. The Hornet is four hours old and we are not used to each other yet. Symbiosis takes time.

Red Hornet and I cross the street and climb Laguna. I notice that I have scratched Hornet already. I apologize to him. We ascend Cathedral Hill, the place where the Catholics, Lutherans, Presbyterians, and Unitarians breathe a collective prayer over my apartment building. I am grateful for this. I unlock my door.

Almost

Tonight, I need to see him. I need to see the sweet MUNI driver with the sexy build and huge arms, the one who calls me "Baby." He says this, not in a sleazy way, or a patronizing way, but in a kind and real way, like he means it. "How ya doin' tonight, baby?" he says softly, always making me smile. He's the only driver I've met where if he asked me out for a drink sometime, I would say yes. I haven't seen him in over six months and I fear he's transferred to another line. I took a restroom break at four today and blindly left the building like I was going home, without my coat, bag, anything, heading for the bus stop. I was halfway down the block before I realized what was happening. I decided that Red Hornet was trying to tell me something. I returned to the office and prepared to cut out early. Just as I shut down my computer, my internal line rang. "Legal Affairs for Nicole" my caller ID said. I rebooted. I was not going home early tonight.

Most of my men friends in San Francisco are gay or unavailable. They are some of the best friends I've ever had, and for a long time, this is what I needed. These relationships are safe, platonic; I am free, theoretically, from the risks of romantic rejection. But for the last six months I've felt a shift in me; I need something else now. I am tired, and need to hear it. Call me Baby. Please.

Red Hornet and I are at the stop now, work duties complete. The bus comes. I squint up the hill. It is not him. I like this driver, though; he is kind and optimistic. I'll get it right this time, he smiles. I've been stuck on the wheelchair lift with him before. He parked on uneven ground, but was very apologetic about it. I'm sure you will, I smile back.

I am in a daze until Fillmore and Eddy. A woman in her mid-twenties tramps on and lowers the window by her seat.

"Hey, where ya goin?" her friend yells from the sidewalk, running up Fillmore toward the bus.

"Booty call!"

"OooOOOO, girl!" the friend shouts in shrill crescendo. "OOOoo-ooo-oo," her hands on her hips.

"I'm gonna get me that man!"

"You go, girlfriend!"

"Better believe it!" she laughs.

We pull out of the stop. Good for her. Perhaps I will go where she is going.

WAITING

I'm taking a risk tonight. The Balboa line between 6:30 and 9:00 p.m. is a crap-shoot. It might come in a timely manner, it might not. It might be okay. I've had timeliness karma so far this year; I haven't yet waited more than five minutes for the bus since I came back from Wisconsin. It might be okay, tonight.

John is walking toward me, and I am glad. John falls in the "gay or unavailable male friend" category—it doesn't matter which, really. John landed on Planet Platonica with the rest of my entourage some time ago and once you land there, you cannot leave. If you leave, you cannot return. One of the best lost his footing in 1998, he slipped off for just a second, and was lost to the Abyss forever. I am still recovering. Leaving Platonica is high risk.

John is a good one, though, and well worth obtaining Platonica visitation rights for. He is a native New Yorker; as I get older my affinity for people who say what they mean increases.

"Hello, Nicole, I haven't seen you in forever," John says, and launches forward. "How was Christmas? How is work? Are you still taking classes? I'm taking a screenwriting class downtown. My job is good. I'm going to stay here for at least another year but I miss my sister. I saw *Gangs of New York* but didn't like it, liked *Chicago* though. Have you seen *Chicago*?" We chat happily for fifteen minutes. Twenty minutes. Thirty minutes.

"I think I've jinxed your MUNI karma," he says.

"Naw, I'm glad for your company," I say.

"You know I was talking to a 38 driver the other day and she told me you can predict exactly when your bus is going to come by marking seven minutes from the time the bus crosses in the opposite direction. I told her there's no way the buses were on this close of a schedule, and she was like, 'Oh, you better believe it we are on a schedule, seven minutes.' So I tested her theory the next time, and she was right. Exactly seven minutes."

"No way."

"Uh-huh."

"Not six minutes or eight minutes?"

"Seven minutes. Looked at my watch twice."

"Wow." I thought about what life would be like if things were always this predictable, predictable as a seven-minute schedule, predictable as John is good company. I do not know this life.

Then three buses come, fifteen minutes later. John gets on the first bus. I know this driver; he is a cross between the Swearing Driver and the Defeatist Driver and never pulls up to the flat part of the sidewalk, even though I sit and wave from there every time. The lift lowers crooked and won't raise at all. Stuck. "Want me to take the next one?" I say. He grunts.

The next bus says "Ask Driver For Terminal." Translation: not my stop. The third bus pulls over but his electric poles fall down as he does this. I can see him swear from inside. John hops off the first bus. "I'll keep you company," he says. God bless John.

The poles are fixed and the lift is lowered, and for a moment the lift is stuck and I hold my breath because John and I are the only ones using this bus and now he'll quite possibly be detained indefinitely because of me. But after one more try all is well and I rise into the bus. I exhale. John hops on, and we are on our way—fifty-two minutes later than when we started.

"My sister was in *Joseph and the Amazing Technicolor Dreamcoat*," he says.

"Really?" I say.

"Yeah, she was great. I saw a tape of it," he says. "She has cerebral palsy like you, have I told you that?"

"I remember," I say.

"Well, not like yours, or like you . . ."

"I know what you mean," I smile.

"Yeah. I really miss her," John says.

Rote Hornisse

Gerold taught me how to say "Red Hornet" in German last night. I practised a few times. *Rote Hornisse*. WROTE-uh Hor-NISS-uh. Rote Hornisse. It sounds better when Gerold says it. Looks better, too, especially when he has a glass of wine in one hand and a cigarette in the other. Gerold is from Germany and knows swank. I thanked him for the lesson.

I get to leave work early today, but am running late. "C'mon, Rote Hornisse, go fast!" I say. I turn the corner at Masonic and wait at the stop. I have a meeting on Cathedral Hill at four o'clock. With luck, I may be on time.

I wait ten minutes until three packed buses pull up, each behind the other. My best option, given time, is the Geary Limited, the third in line, the fewest number of stops. I wave and the driver pulls over to the sidewalk. The bus patrons exhale a collective groan.

"We don't have time to pick her up!" one of the patrons shouts from the rear. Collective agreement. I exhale. I wait.

"Well, I have all the time in the world!" the driver says, pointing to her chest. "So the sooner y'all get out of her way, the sooner we'll be movin'."

Silence.

"I'm serious. I'm not movin' 'til y'all move for her."

I smile. Folks begin to shuffle back, slowly. *Watch out, or Rote Hornisse will squash you!* I think.

"See what happens with a little cooperation?" the driver says. She lowers the wheelchair lift.

On the way out, I tell the driver she is nice. Rote Hornisse says danke, too.

Looking for Port Hardy

Jacyntha England

Early one evening at the end of August 1980, just when other people's fathers are coming home to turn on their sprinklers and barbecues, my father and I leave a house on the outskirts of Prince George and head west to the coast on Highway 16. The house belongs to my mother and it is the only place I have ever lived.

"The Inside Passage, god that's something else, mountains coming right out of the water. Been wanting to take that trip again for years," he says as he turns the key in the ignition.

I am twelve, and the last time I saw my father was six years ago. Now I guess he's decided it's time for a reunion and is taking me on a fishing trip to Port Hardy, someplace over on Vancouver Island. I know this is where we are going because I heard my mom talking to him on the phone last night, calling him an asshole and complaining about him taking me someplace way the hell in the middle of nowhere just when school is about to start.

We roll down the windows and drive for hours along the highway, Dad singing along to the radio whenever it plays a Neil Young song. I fall asleep around midnight, and a couple of hours later Dad wakes me up to show me the moon shining on the Skeena River. We take off our shoes and dip our toes in the icy rapids, where the moonlight makes the water look like moving crystals. He lets me sip his coffee and laughs when I spit it out.

It's still dark when we reach Prince Rupert, and I'm too sleepy to notice that we've hit the end of the mainland. Dad pulls into the ferry terminal, parks behind a line of trucks and tells me he's going for a walk. He comes back with a coffee for him and a pop and bag of chips for me. It starts to rain and I doze off, waking to find us inching up a ramp into a cave of flashing lights and echoing whistles. The ferry's enormous steel doors close just behind us, sealing me off from the only home I have ever known.

Twelve hours later I am beginning to think my mom made a mistake in letting me come on this trip. It has done nothing but rain since we set sail, so now the passenger lounge smells of wet socks and all the kids younger than me are crying. I want to go to the bathroom but am afraid to leave Dad, who is asleep on the floor. The ferry chairs were hurting his back so he spread out in the aisle, and now he is snoring and people have to keep stepping over him. He seems so sad lying there, with his greasy hair and wrinkled shirt, so I pretend I don't know him when people complain that he is blocking their path.

The deck looks ravaged and inhospitable now, like a science fiction movie set meant to resemble Earth after a nuclear bomb. Two smokers straggle outside, small and weak against the backdrop of rain and fog. One of them, a girl, wears high heels that make her slip on the wet floor. I think she is crying. They huddle miserably beside a garbage can, trying to keep a match lit long enough to light their cigarettes. An announcer comes on the loudspeaker and says that the ferry is making progress, but due to the high winds is not expected to reach Port Hardy for at least another two hours. The listless passengers barely even raise their heads from their books and card games. Maybe they are beginning to think, like me, that this so-called Port Hardy doesn't really exist, that it is only some fictitious, imagined harbour our struggling ship will never find. Dad rolls over onto his side and snores even louder. I bite my lip to keep from falling asleep.

Then someone cries out "Whales! Over there! See?" Four gigantic killer whales have appeared out of the fog, leaping and slapping their tails in the waves. Against the grey of the water their backs look like shiny black jewels, their white bellies close enough to touch. All the passengers crowd to our side of the ship, pulling out binoculars and cameras and lifting their kids to the window. The commotion wakes my dad, and he gestures to me to follow him. We head out onto the deck, the wind whipping our hair into our eyes, the rain dripping down the backs of our necks. We are the only ones out there, but I can feel the eyes of those still inside boring into us from behind. I think maybe they recognize us as the ones who were blocking their way in the aisle, and now they are pissed off because we're blocking their view of the whales.

Dad sways on his feet and puts an arm around my shoulder. "I think they might be laughing at us, those whales. I mean, we must look pretty funny up here to them," he grins.

I had forgotten he has a gap between his teeth when he smiles. I look around—at the fog, the whales, the geeky way Dad's hair has begun to curl in the rain—and burst into a giggle. In a moment Dad is laughing too, doubling over and stamping his feet in the puddles. We laugh so hard we have to hold onto each other to keep from falling, so hard we forget about the rain, the mountains we didn't see, the other passengers and what they might think of us. We laugh because we might never be together on a ferry, in the rain, again.

The TTC Chronicles

Patricia Rutale

1978: Watch Out for Leg Slashers

The Simpsons-Sears head office building on Jarvis Street is shaped like an upside-down wedding cake. At 4:30 p.m., Monday to Friday, the secretaries rush out in a mob to catch the Dundas streetcar.

I've just moved to Toronto. It's my first real job. I wear a skirt or a dress, and high heels. I hurry with the other women. The streetcar makes a mighty racket from way down the street, screeching and grinding, traffic fighting around its bulk like a herd of smaller animals. It's always packed, and stinky at the end of the day, but I'm still excited about everything.

The Warwick Hotel, not yet in demolition history, is across the road from the stop. A fat woman with messy black hair hangs around all the time asking for money and cigarettes. One day I'm late, waiting by myself, and when I say I don't have any change, she starts yelling, "Whore! Blonde bitch!" A couple of weeks later, when I give her a cigarette, she's polite: "Thanks a lot, eh." We light up together.

"That wasn't very nice," I say, "what you called me before."

"That wasn't me," she says.

"It was so," I say.

She steps closer. "THAT WASN'T ME!"

I decide to let it go this time.

I feel lucky to get this job since I haven't got any secretarial training. I didn't even take typing in school, so I'm not very good yet, and worse at Dictaphone, but my boss says with those legs he can forgive a lot. He's old, with greasy hair and rabbity teeth. Remarks like that gross me out. He's not the only one. "The guys like watching you put your boots on," a woman explains during the winter when I can't figure out why there's always a crowd in front of the drinking fountain. These are men thirty years old and more, with wives and kids. I've never seen my father behave this way. I start putting my boots on in the bathroom.

Then a story goes around that someone is slashing the backs of women's legs as they get on streetcars around the city. Because it's so cold, the women don't know anything is wrong until they thaw a little, feel the pain, and realize blood is pouring down the backs of their legs. I never discover if it's true or just another urban legend. But I start taking note of who's behind me, and going up the steps fast.

We're packed in tight one hot summer afternoon, swaying together like a colony of deep-sea plankton. It's an old "Red Rocket," the walls tin thin, all the windows open, car exhaust mixing with body odour. At least my feet aren't sore. I've been sitting on my bum all day, the way I generally do, adding up columns of figures, typing letters to suppliers outlining the schedule for the next catalogue.

A large woman holds plastic bags bulging with groceries in both hands, these holding her down so she doesn't have to hang on to the straps overhead. The stink of a fresh fart takes to the air. Everyone looks disgusted. A boy in glasses reading a book by the window smiles and says, "Excuse me." Suddenly the horn blares, we screech to a stop, and the woman is hurled forward, never letting go of her bags. She lands on one of my fashionable high-heeled sandals. My foot swells to the size of a meat loaf. I have to stay home for a week, but nothing is broken.

I start leaving dress shoes at work, and walking the ten blocks from my apartment in track shoes. I also start wearing pants.

1980: You Have to Be Careful

I live with my boyfriend in a one-bedroom at Victoria Park and Danforth, in a group of high rises called Crescent Town. Every morning, I merge with the stream of bodies crossing the skywalk to the Victoria Park subway, which is above ground and open at both ends. It's cold in bad weather, but near the east end of the Bloor-Danforth line, so there's a good chance of getting a seat in the mornings. It's a long stretch downtown, and I can get some reading accomplished.

A blind woman lives in our building. She goes to work around the same time I do, walking fast with everyone else, white cane tapping back and forth. She sits reading with her fingers, face tilted up, eyes behind dark glasses.

The subway cars are usually clean and graffiti free. By now I've been told that they're not that way in other places, and I should be grateful. Ads run in a banner over the windows. Smoking is permitted on platforms even in the stations that are underground. Lighting up will often make the subway train appear.

My mild high-school habit has turned into a pack-a-day addiction. But I'm not concerned, figuring I can always quit when I'm twenty-five. I like the way the silver package looks sitting on my desk. Half the staff smokes in the hermetically sealed building, a powerful ventilation system sucking the smoke out from over the desks. The odd non-smoker complains, but not too loudly, not yet. One day my little calendar catches fire, and I freeze. The woman at the next desk puts it out with her shoe. We laugh and she describes how my face turned white.

My boyfriend doesn't smoke or take the TTC. He works for a steel company in a western suburb, and drives an old silver Mustang that's constantly breaking down. At our apartment, he parks underground where the areas are labelled with different animals. When there's a series of sexual attacks down there, he talks about dressing up like a woman and teaching someone a lesson. I'm opposed, plus I don't believe it will work. He never does it anyway.

In the lighted caverns of the subway, I feel safe, despite being surrounded by strangers and strangeness. A tall delicate man, languid and preoccupied, pirouettes from one end of the car to the other. A chunky girl in flowered sunglasses speaks angrily to someone sitting beside her, but no one is there. A leather-clad couple either has sex, or pretends to, in a back corner. A bald man with a goatee sings *Rock me gent-ly, rock me slowowly* . . . , closing his eyes, holding an invisible microphone. A woman wearing a black evening gown at eight in the morning smiles at me, showing plastic fangs. At least I assume they're plastic.

There are many more weird people in Toronto than in the much smaller city I come from. When I go home for holidays my family enjoys hearing about them, so I become a sort of collector of weird people.

I give my seat to pregnant women, the disabled (not yet called "physically challenged"), and old people. That's my policy. But the blind woman doesn't like it at all. It really makes her mad. She looks like she wants to hit me across the face with her cane, which leads me to think about other ways kindness might offend, and after that I'm more careful.

1981: Getting a Front Seat

My eleven-year-old brother comes for the weekend. He sleeps in the bed with me. My boyfriend sleeps on the sofa. We make up a story about how his place is getting sprayed for roaches. It isn't known officially by my family that we're living together.

My brother doesn't care much about where anyone is sleeping. It's his first time here, and he's wild about Toronto. He wants to go to the Eaton Centre, ride the escalators, purchase a new *Star Wars* action figure in the toy department upstairs, see a movie at the Imperial Six, and have dinner at Mr. Greenjeans. My mother has given me money for all this.

He can't wait to ride the "Silver Bullet." I've already issued warnings: "Don't get too close to the edge," "Stay back until it stops," "Watch the gap when you get in."

On the platform he jumps up and down. "Here it comes! Here it comes! It sounds like thunder!" He's awestruck when it shoots into the station. "Space age," he says. He wants to sit in the first seat of the first car.

There's already someone in that seat, an Asian boy on his knees at the window. My brother looks at me as if I should throw this kid out bodily. I point out there's room for him, too. When the car starts to move he goes and kneels cautiously beside the other boy. The speed picks up, the car moves into the tunnel, and he starts smiling, looking down at the tracks, into the tunnel ahead, and at the other boy as if they're on a ride.

After a few stops, he wants to see inside the closet-sized room where the driver is. The window is covered but he knocks on the glass, assuming anyone would be thrilled to meet him. Luckily the man who opens the door likes kids, smiles, and shows both boys the controls. I look in, too—the secrets of the little room. There's not much to it. It would be boring as hell, unless someone jumped, then it *would* be hell.

I've got to do something else with my life. At Sears, lots of men without university degrees have worked their way up, but the rare female executive commonly has a MBA and nerves of steel. I fear the lives of the women I work with in the clerical pool—kids and mortgages, riding the Go Train in from the suburbs five days a week to work in the upside-down wedding cake until retirement. I see how easily the wedding cake can turn.

1983: I Just Sit There

A group of white teenage girls and a group of black teenage girls stand on opposite sides of the subway car. "Your face looks like shit," a white girl says to a black girl.

"Yours looks like toilet paper," the black girl says. Then all the black girls laugh like crazy, and the white girls scowl dangerously.

I've gotten married, and turned twenty-three in Europe where we country hopped by train and spent all the wedding money. Now I'm going to the downtown campus of the University of Toronto. I take the subway to Spadina, and then get on the bus.

On my way home one day, a black man gets on the bus and sits up front by the driver. He asks how to get to Bloor and Christie. "I can't understand you," the driver says. The black man is young and slender, wearing a green T-shirt and jeans. He repeats himself politely and smiles. The driver shakes his head. "I can't understand a damn word you're saying." The young man has a Jamaican accent, but I think what he's saying is clear enough.

It's mid-afternoon. The bus is almost empty. A woman sitting up front repeats "Bloor and Christie," aiming her voice at the driver. The bus stops, the doors open, a couple of kids jump on and head to the back. The driver continues on as if he didn't hear a thing. The woman looks around helplessly. "I'm sorry," she says to the man, "I don't know how to get there."

I think Christie might be a subway stop. I'm not sure, but I'm *thinking* about doing something, about saying something to the driver, like, "You heard him, what's the matter with you?" Even though he might tell me to get off—they can do that. I'm thinking very hard when a young man, probably also a student, who has been thinking either harder or quicker than I have, walks forward against the motion of the bus and sits down beside the black man. He tells the man that Christie is on the Bloor West line, he's going in that direction himself, and that he'll need a transfer to take a bus from there. The student plucks a transfer from the driver, who keeps staring straight ahead. The black man smiles as if this makes everything all right. "Thank you, man, I just got here."

"And now you probably think everybody is a prick," says the student.

1987: I Don't Just Sit There

I'm travelling west on the subway with my head bent, studying physiology, but not too anxious about this one. I'm in my third year of pharmacy. Second year was crazy with ten subjects, eight with labs, but this year is a breeze with six subjects and only two labs.

We bought a house just before I went back to school, an East York bungalow that needed some work, and still needs it. My husband now works for a contracting company and has a company truck, but we're still constantly broke with me going to school all this time. I'm getting sick of studying, and even sicker of having no money, but the typing life is still fresh in my mind.

A body sits down beside me. I wonder why this is, with all the other seats in the section empty. "Hi there." A man about my age, clean cut, clean white teeth smiling at me. "You a student?" I nod and look back into my book. He keeps trying to talk.

"I need to study," I tell him.

"You should smile once in a while," he says. "I'm just trying to be friendly."

I stop responding.

"What's your problem, sweetheart?"

I shut the book, look around and take stock. It's a car with no driver, but several passengers are seated in the next section. I stand up.

"Hey, relax," he says, "I just wanted to talk to a pretty girl."

I push out of the seat, already thinking *make a lot of noise*, when he grabs the strap of my bag. "GET YOUR FUCKING HANDS OFF ME!"

He's on his feet, too, looking as if he was just some innocent guy minding his own business. "She's nuts," he tells the people with their chins up staring at us. He gets off when the doors open and stands glaring. As the car rolls out, he thrashes his tongue around like a rock singer. I give him both middle fingers.

1988: Can You Smell the Manure Yet?

I graduate and pass the provincial licensing exams. I'm a pharmacist, and excited about everything. Yes, again. I never learn. There are lots of jobs. I could go almost anywhere in the province. My husband grew up in Toronto, and now he wants out. We want more space, some land, clean air, nature. At least at the moment this is what we think we want. We sell our house and buy another one on a quarter acre on the outskirts of a farm town with a population of twelve thousand where I've found a job. Only an hour's drive from Toronto, but a vastly different place. Let me tell you.

So we are about to discover a few pitfalls of small towns and rural living, among other things. There's no public transit in this town, not even a bus. At age twenty-nine, I buy my own car and begin the Chrysler chronicles.

Sometime this year, I must have taken my last ride on the TTC. I can't remember a thing about it.

AFTERWORD

Bus Riders Are Part of the Big Picture

David Suzuki

There's a game I like to play whenever I'm waiting at a bus stop. I count the number of cars that go by with only one person in them. By the time my bus arrives, I've usually lost count. Try it sometime. It's easy to see that we're not doing a very good job of getting people out of their cars and onto public transit.

There are hard numbers to back up my unscientific sidewalk survey. According to data from the 1996 census, 8.9 million people—that's seventy-three per cent of the Canadian workforce—drove to work as the single occupant of a vehicle, while only ten per cent commuted by public transit, seven per cent carpooled, another seven per cent walked, and two per cent bicycled. Not only do most Canadians drive to work, fewer and fewer of us are choosing to take public transportation. Federal numbers show public transit usage has actually decreased by thirteen per cent since 1990!

Why do so many Canadians avoid the bus? Part of the problem is a lack of federal funding. As a result, our transit systems aren't fast enough or convenient enough or direct enough to make them attractive options for more people. Because there aren't enough riders on certain routes to make it financially worthwhile for transit authorities, service is reduced or bus lines are cancelled altogether.

Cheap gasoline and other fossil fuels have been around long enough for us to build a huge infrastructure based on them. Our cities are decentralized and, lacking adequate public transit, people often have no choice but to drive. Meanwhile, the auto industry spends billions marketing the "safety" and convenience of gas-guzzling SUVs.

But there is a way out. We have to start looking at the environment as something we are part of rather than something we live in. When we dump vast quantities of pollutants into our air, water, and soil, they do not simply disappear. The earth can only absorb so much and we've well surpassed those limits in many areas.

Cars have a bad reputation when it comes to the environment —and deservedly so. Of all transportation modes (automobiles, planes, buses, trains, and ferries), cars are the biggest culprits, causing the most carbon dioxide emissions, causing urban blight with enormous road infrastructure, and polluting our air and water through exhaust, road runoff, and waste from auto maintenance and manufacturing.

Driving is the most polluting thing that we as individuals do. Car exhaust is a significant source of pollutants, including carbon monoxide, oxides of nitrogen, ozone, volatile organic compounds, and small airborne particulates. These air pollutants contribute to a wide range of health problems including impaired lung function, shortness of breath, wheezing, and asthma attacks.

One of the most serious consequences of our addiction to the automobile is that it causes global warming. When we burn vast amounts of gasoline—or any other fossil fuel—we're producing carbon dioxide and altering the chemical composition of the atmosphere. And when we alter the atmosphere, we're tampering with the planet's ability to support the intricate balance of life.

Many plants and animals face extinction as a result of global warming. Drastic changes in habitats will mean that some species will not be able to migrate quickly enough to survive. Scientists are already reporting serious changes in the polar bear population in the eastern Canadian Arctic. Warmer Arctic weather patterns are causing earlier ice break-up and are affecting the feeding habits of the bears, who need the ice as a platform to hunt for seals.

Climate change is also expected to cause more droughts, floods, heat waves, severe storms, and worse urban smog across Canada.

How do we solve this problem? One of the solutions is to change the way we build our communities. Cities have generally taken one of two strategies to reduce traffic: building more roads and parking garages, or investing in more efficient public transit. Yet the first strategy—building more auto-related infrastructure—is no solution at all. More roads mean more cars and eventually the result is more traffic congestion, increased greenhouse gas emissions, and worse air pollution. By contrast, a single public bus takes forty vehicles off the road during rush hour, saves 70,000 litres of fuel, and reduces air pollutants by nine tonnes a year.

Streets should work for pedestrians and cyclists as well as cars. Better urban planning would also lead to more efficient transit systems for commuters. Public transit must be planned to knit various neighbourhoods together. To achieve this, municipal governments could support mass transit lines such as buses, subways, and light rail, while instituting traffic calming measures and greenways that make walking and biking easier.

Better planning will reduce greenhouse gas emissions, as well as improve regional and local air quality, ease road congestion, and reduce both unproductive commuting time and municipal infrastructure costs.

Increasing public transit usage and infrastructure will improve urban growth management, thereby reducing the impacts of urban sprawl. As commercial centres and more compact residential developments occur along transit lines, the amount of land dedicated to urban areas is reduced. Additionally, as fewer cars are on the road and congestion decreases, less land is needed for new roads. In cities that practice compact growth management, the amount of land needed for urban areas decreases dramatically, as do municipal infrastructure costs. For example, the population of Portland, Oregon, has grown by fifty per cent over the last twenty years yet the urban area has expanded by only two per cent, while Chicago's population grew by four per cent but used forty-six per cent more land over the same period.

We also know that when action is taken, public health improves. For example, when Atlanta put strict driving rules in effect for the 1996 Summer Olympics, air pollution dropped. Fleets of buses and public transit around the clock resulted in a drastic reduction in traffic density and the amount of vehicle exhaust during the seventeen days that Atlanta hosted the Olympics. A report published in the *Journal of the American Medical Association* shows asthma-related emergency visits and hospitalizations decreased about forty per cent. Ozone dropped almost thirty per cent during the Olympics, and asthma attacks among children in the city plummeted dramatically—forty-two per cent.

These data provide support for efforts to reduce air pollution and improve health via reductions in motor vehicle traffic.

Not only does better public transit reduce the need for sprawl, it's easier on your wallet. In 1999, the Canadian Automobile Association estimated the annual cost of owning and operating a full-size car was $11,500. An alternative commuting plan will cost much less. A Toronto study estimated that the annual cost of alternative transportation was $5,600, which included an unlimited TTC pass, car rental for two weekends a month, and two taxi rides a week.

But to realistically get people out of their cars, it's critical to improve the attractiveness, frequency, and convenience of transit services. Our buses, streetcars, and subways must be more reliable and convenient. It's easy to tell people about the environmental and economic benefits of taking public transit. But when they have to walk a kilometre to get to a bus stop and then spend twenty minutes in the pouring rain waiting for a bus that is uncomfortably packed when it finally arrives way behind schedule, it's not that easy to convince someone to change.

So how do we go about making public transit better? More money would be a good start. Currently, local and provincial governments spend nearly $3 billion per year on transit, while the federal government provides no funding. In fact, Canada is the only Western industrialized country in which the national government provides no funding for transit. In order to revitalize transit in Canada, the federal government should establish a public transit improvement fund aimed at upgrading and expanding transit out of annual fuel tax revenue.

Another way to convince more people to leave the car at home is to allow employer-subsidized transit passes to be a non-taxable benefit. Employees who receive free parking rights from employers do not have to declare this benefit as income, creating a tax subsidy for parking. At the same time, if an employee receives a transit pass it must be declared as income, creating a transit pass tax penalty. In Canada, it is estimated that removing the tax penalty for transit passes will result in a further five per cent of single occupant travellers changing their mode of transportation for commuting by 2010.

By providing transit funding, removing tax penalties against employee-sponsored transit passes, and supporting alternative modes of transportation, government help can reverse the trend toward single-passenger vehicle use.

Albert Einstein said, "We cannot solve the problems that we have created with the same thinking that created them." By taking action as individuals and governments to make public transit a priority, we will show we have a sense of responsibility beyond our lifetime to the future generations of Canadians.

ABOUT THE AUTHORS

JEREMIAH AHERNE is a MFA grad from UBC currently biding his time in Point Roberts, WA. He is an ardent supporter of public transit in all forms, although since living on "The Point" he has only caught the bus into the city once. There are limits, some fares too high.

NICOLE BOHN, a northern Wisconsin native, has lived in San Francisco since 1996. A creative non-fiction writer and poet, Nicole's day job finds her working as an advocate and administrator for college students with disabilities. She obtained a MA in Counseling in 1998, and a MFA in Writing in 2002, from the University of San Francisco. This is her first publication.

MARC BOUDIGNON works as a film editor in Toronto, where he rides the "Red Rocket" daily. He has written album reviews and interviews for www.uttermusic.com and his poetry has appeared in the Toronto Small Press Book Fair's *Instant Anthology*. He is currently working on his first novel.

IAN COCKFIELD is the editor of this volume of commuter literature. You can find out more about him on the back cover.

JACYNTHA ENGLAND is a writer, traveller, and educator who has lived and worked in Europe, Asia, Africa, and the Caribbean. She is a recent graduate of The Writers Studio at SFU and is currently completing a MA in Educational Studies at UBC. Her writing has appeared in *subTerrain*, *The New Quarterly* and various academic journals.

Matthew Firth was born and raised in Hamilton and now lives in Ottawa. He is the author of two short story collections: *Fresh Meat* and *Can You Take Me There, Now?* He is co-editor of *Grunt and Groan: The New Fiction Anthology of Work and Sex.* He also edits/publishes the new fiction/review publication *Front&Centre* and is editor of Black Bile Press. He works by day for a national trade union and can be contacted at firth@istar.ca

Ariel Gordon is a Winnipeg-based writer and editor. After spending several years as a "come-from-away" and a "foreign-devil," she returned to Winnipeg in 1999. Since then, she has tried her hand at a novel, several poetry manuscripts, and six varieties of non-fiction. Her work has recently appeared in *Room of One's Own* and *Pottersfield Portfolio,* and is forthcoming in *Contemporary Verse 2, Lichen*, and the Manitoba Writers' Guild's *Poetry Fix* project. Besides pining for a book with her name on it, Ariel sits on the boards of *Prairie Fire* and the MWG.

Scott Gunning lives in Calgary. His works have appeared in a number of the city's pubs and include "The Cosmopolitan" and the coming-of-age piece, "The Vodka Paralyzer." Scott has written for *Fast Forward* magazine and presented work in collaboration with local choreographers at Dancers' Studio West.

Matt Hern lives with his partner and daughters in east Vancouver. He runs the Purple Thistle Centre, an alternative-to-school youth project and edits *Crank* magazine. He holds a PhD in Urban Studies, is a faculty member at the Institute for Social Ecology and remains obsessed with sports in general and boxing in particular. His new book about education is called *Field Day* (New Star).

KEVIN IRIE has published three books of poetry: *Burning the Dead* (Wolsak & Wynn), *The Colour of Eden* (Owl's Head Press)—a finalist for The City of Toronto Book Award—and *Dinner at Madonna's* (Frontenac House). He was born and lives in Toronto.

STEPHEN JOHNSON is a New York City writer. His work has appeared in *Columbia: A Journal of Literature and Art*, *Mr. Beller's Neighborhood*, and *Gadfly*. He is getting his MFA from Columbia and finishing a thesis about urban archeology, decay, and dreams.

KARIN KONOVAL is a professional actor living in Vancouver. Her writing has been broadcast on CBC's "First Person Singular" and "Alberta Anthology," and published in *Other Voices* literary magazine, *Playboard* magazine, and *The Vancouver Courier*.

CHRIS LAVIGNE thinks everybody should ride public transit because we'd all get so much more reading done. Speaking of which, he also thinks everybody should read *The Republic*, an independent Vancouver newspaper for whom he writes a regular arts column. Like all writers, he displays an obvious inclination towards self-promotion and totalitarianism, but his heart is in the right place.

CATHERINE MCNEIL, writer, Teacher of the Deaf, musician, has been published in many anthologies including *The Fed Anthology, Chasing Haley's Comet* and *Tightly Wound,* and magazines such as *Event* and *The Capilano Review*. She has two chapbooks, *the hungry eye* and *mutual notes*, and her first collection of poetry, *under the influence,* was selected for publication by Milieu Press in 2003.

TERESA MCWHIRTER was born in Vancouver and grew up in the East and West Kootenays. After receiving a BA in English/Writing at UVic, she travelled and worked odd jobs while she wrote. Her first book, *Some Girls Do*, was published by Raincoast/Polestar in 2001. She has lived in Vancouver on the lower eastside for several years, and is currently finishing her second manuscript.

ELAINE MILLER, 34, lives in Vancouver. She's been involved in every aspect of literacy except for paper-making, is a published writer of both fiction and non-fiction, and has a regular newspaper column called "Slap and Tickle." She also does too many things for a living, including stage performance, web design and hosting, desktop publishing, make-up artistry, and teaching a variety of subjects on human sexuality.

ALLEN MOORE worked for two decades in high technology. He designed laser writing equipment for the graphic arts industry and instrumentation for astrophysics. Since leaving work two years ago, Allen has become a volunteer in his community. He provides support to people who are suffering with terminal illness.

PETER NORMAN's work has appeared in various periodicals, including *The Malahat Review*, *Vancouver* magazine, and *Event*. A story is included in the anthology *Victory Meat: New Fiction from Atlantic Canada*. His poetry chapbook *After Stillness* is available from above/ground press. He lives in Ottawa with his wife, author Melanie Little.

MATT ROBINSON's second collection is *how we play at it: a list* (ECW Press); his first, *A Ruckus of Awkward Stacking*, was short-listed for the Lampert and ReLit Poetry Awards.

Recipient of The New Brunswick Foundation for the Arts' Emerging Artist of the Year Award for 2003, his poetry has appeared on radio and television and in numerous anthologies. robinson is Poetry Editor at *The Fiddlehead* and President of The League of Canadian Poets.

PATRICIA RUTALE lives, writes, and works as a pharmacist in the city of Guelph, where a public transit system has been in operation since 1895.

DAVID SUZUKI is a renowned Canadian broadcaster and scientist. He is a passionate advocate of environmental protection and public transportation. He lives in Vancouver.

JOHN VIGNA lives in Vancouver where he is at work on his book, *Travels with the Tabla: A Musical Journey across India.*

Exact Fare Only 3?

Even before this volume went to press we were asking ourselves the question, *Should we do it again?*

The well of entertaining, true transit tales seems to be virtually inexhaustible—so why stop now? If you have a good, true tale about travelling on "public transit" then we encourage you to send it in. When we have enough great content to warrant it, we'll issue *Exact Fare Only 3*, another volume of wild, wacky, and humorous commuter literature.

Send your true tales of public transit to:

Exact Fare Only 3
Anvil Press Publishers
PO Box 3008, MPO
Vancouver, BC
V6B 3X5
CANADA